DECORATIVE STENCILS

Projects by Kathryn Collyer
Photography by Stillview Photography
Illustrations by Carol Daniel
Written and created by the Top That! team .

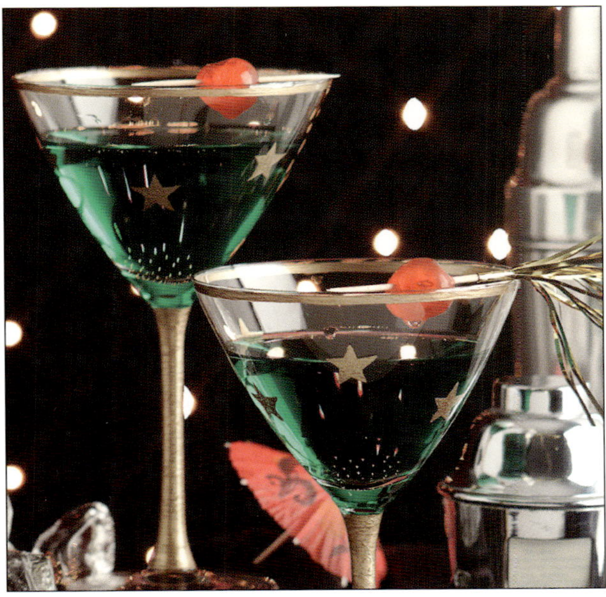

TOP THAT!™

Copyright © 2003 Top That! Publishing plc,
Top That! Publishing 27023 McBean Parkway, #408 Valencia, CA 91355
Top That! is a Registered Trademark of Top That! Publishing plc
All rights reserved
www.topthatpublishing.com

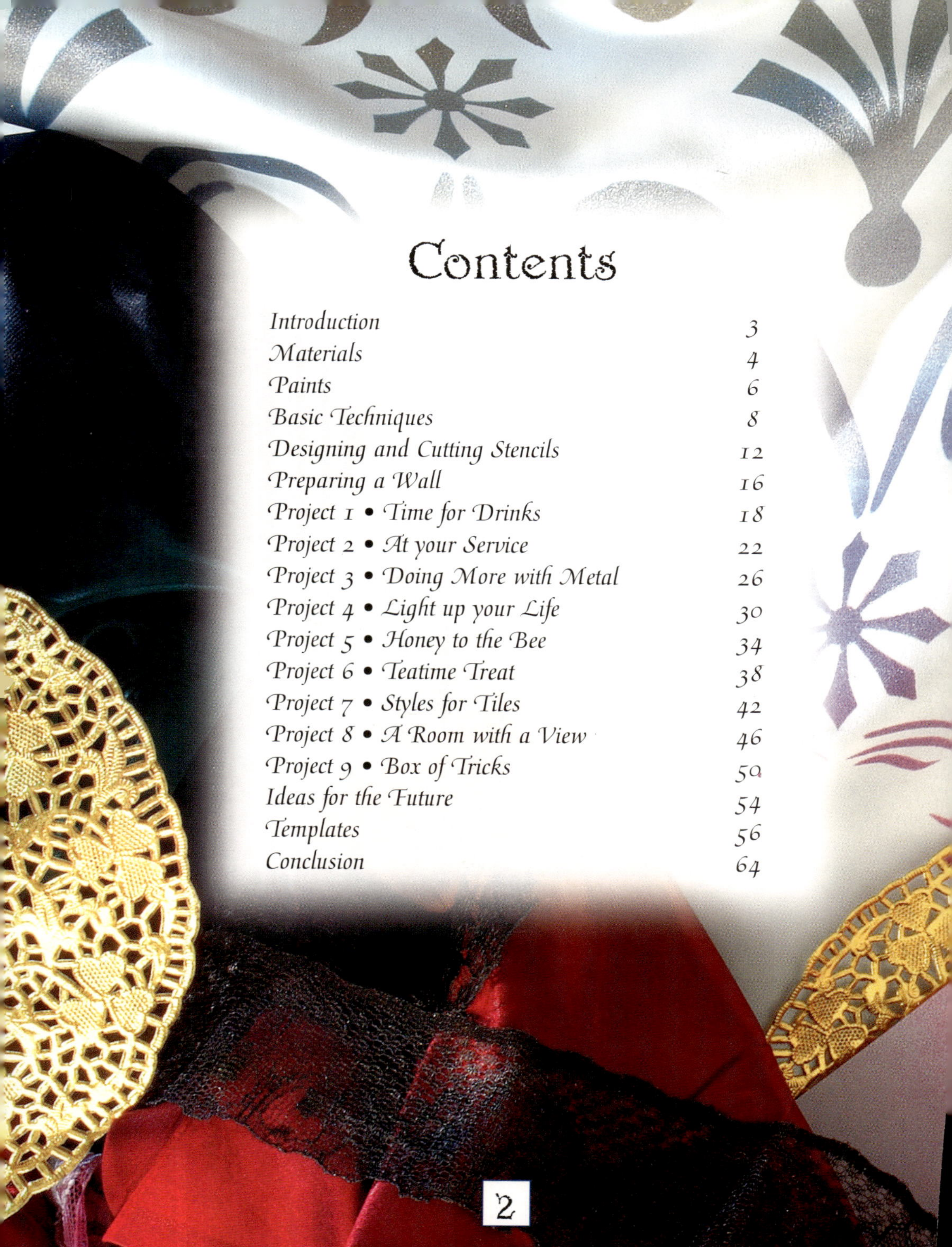

Contents

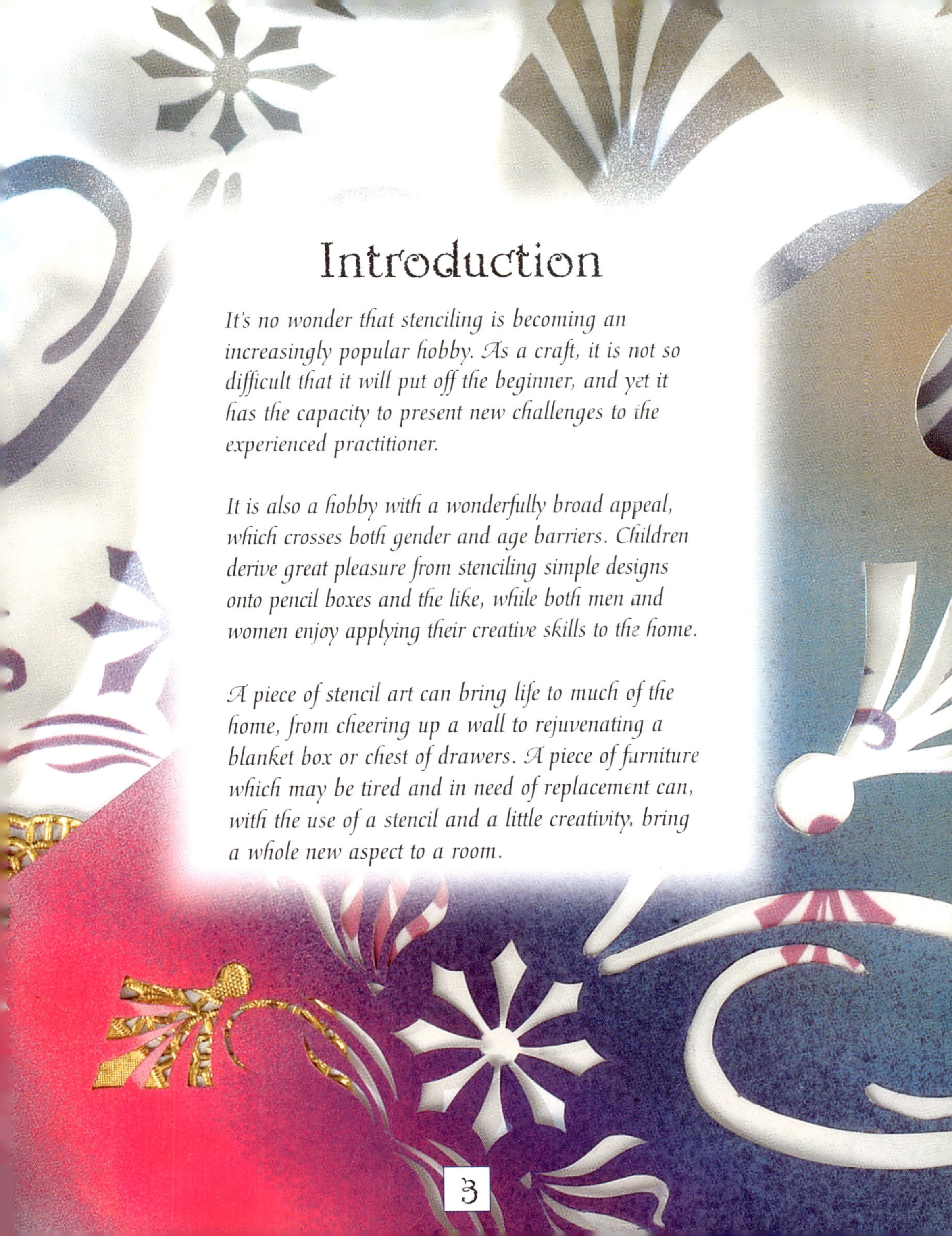

Introduction

It's no wonder that stenciling is becoming an increasingly popular hobby. As a craft, it is not so difficult that it will put off the beginner, and yet it has the capacity to present new challenges to the experienced practitioner.

It is also a hobby with a wonderfully broad appeal, which crosses both gender and age barriers. Children derive great pleasure from stenciling simple designs onto pencil boxes and the like, while both men and women enjoy applying their creative skills to the home.

A piece of stencil art can bring life to much of the home, from cheering up a wall to rejuvenating a blanket box or chest of drawers. A piece of furniture which may be tired and in need of replacement can, with the use of a stencil and a little creativity, bring a whole new aspect to a room.

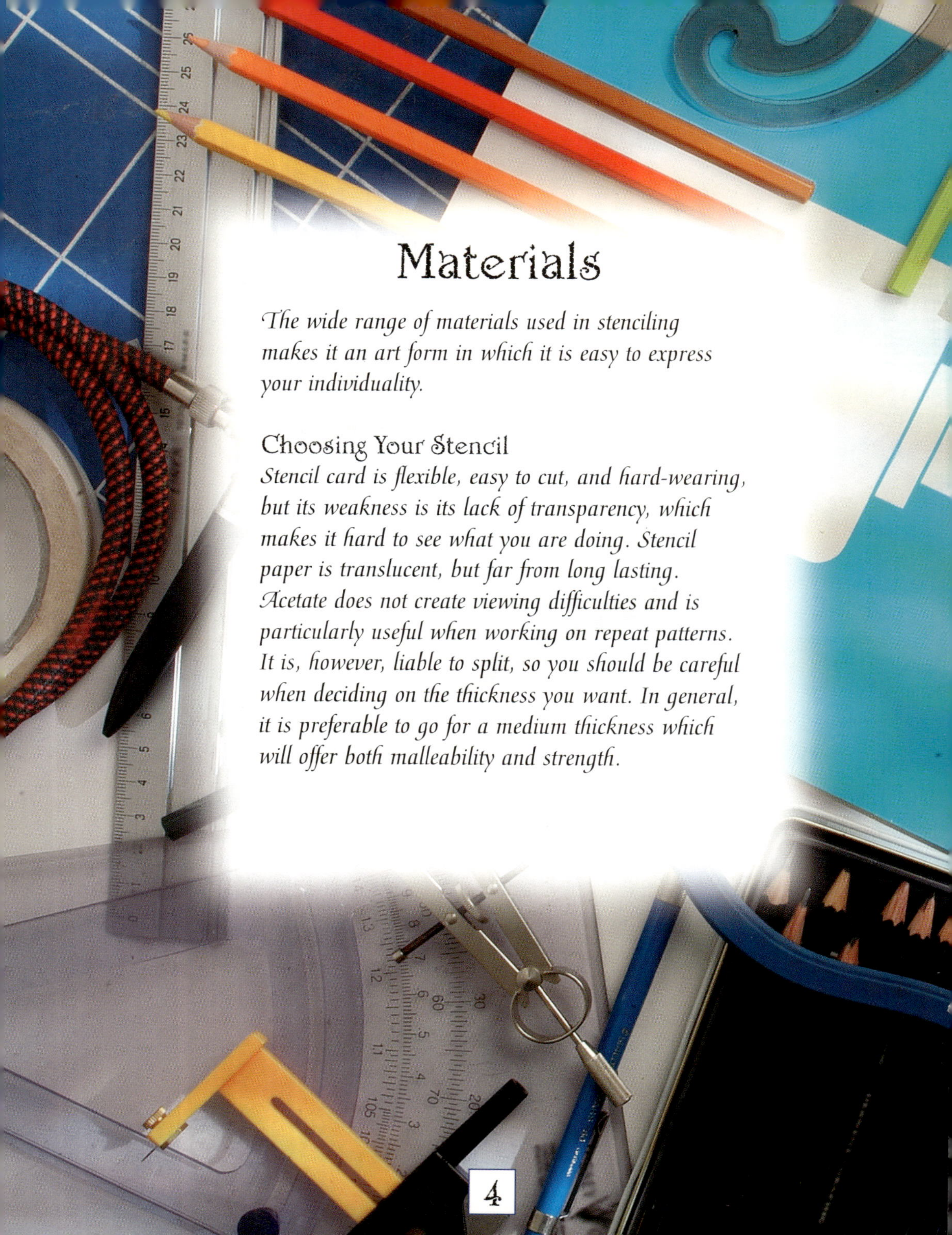

Materials

The wide range of materials used in stenciling makes it an art form in which it is easy to express your individuality.

Choosing Your Stencil

Stencil card is flexible, easy to cut, and hard-wearing, but its weakness is its lack of transparency, which makes it hard to see what you are doing. Stencil paper is translucent, but far from long lasting. Acetate does not create viewing difficulties and is particularly useful when working on repeat patterns. It is, however, liable to split, so you should be careful when deciding on the thickness you want. In general, it is preferable to go for a medium thickness which will offer both malleability and strength.

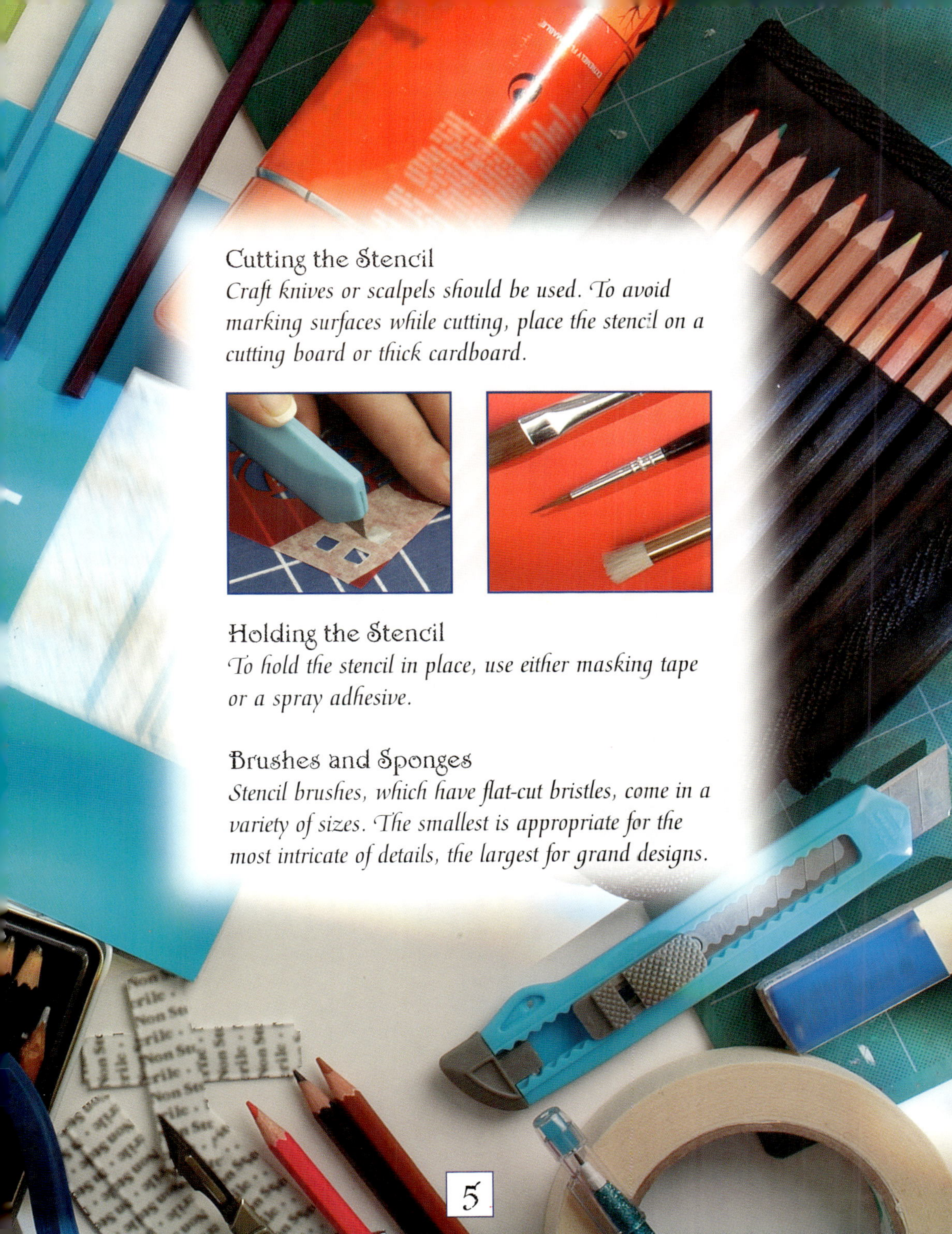

Cutting the Stencil

Craft knives or scalpels should be used. To avoid marking surfaces while cutting, place the stencil on a cutting board or thick cardboard.

Holding the Stencil

To hold the stencil in place, use either masking tape or a spray adhesive.

Brushes and Sponges

Stencil brushes, which have flat-cut bristles, come in a variety of sizes. The smallest is appropriate for the most intricate of details, the largest for grand designs.

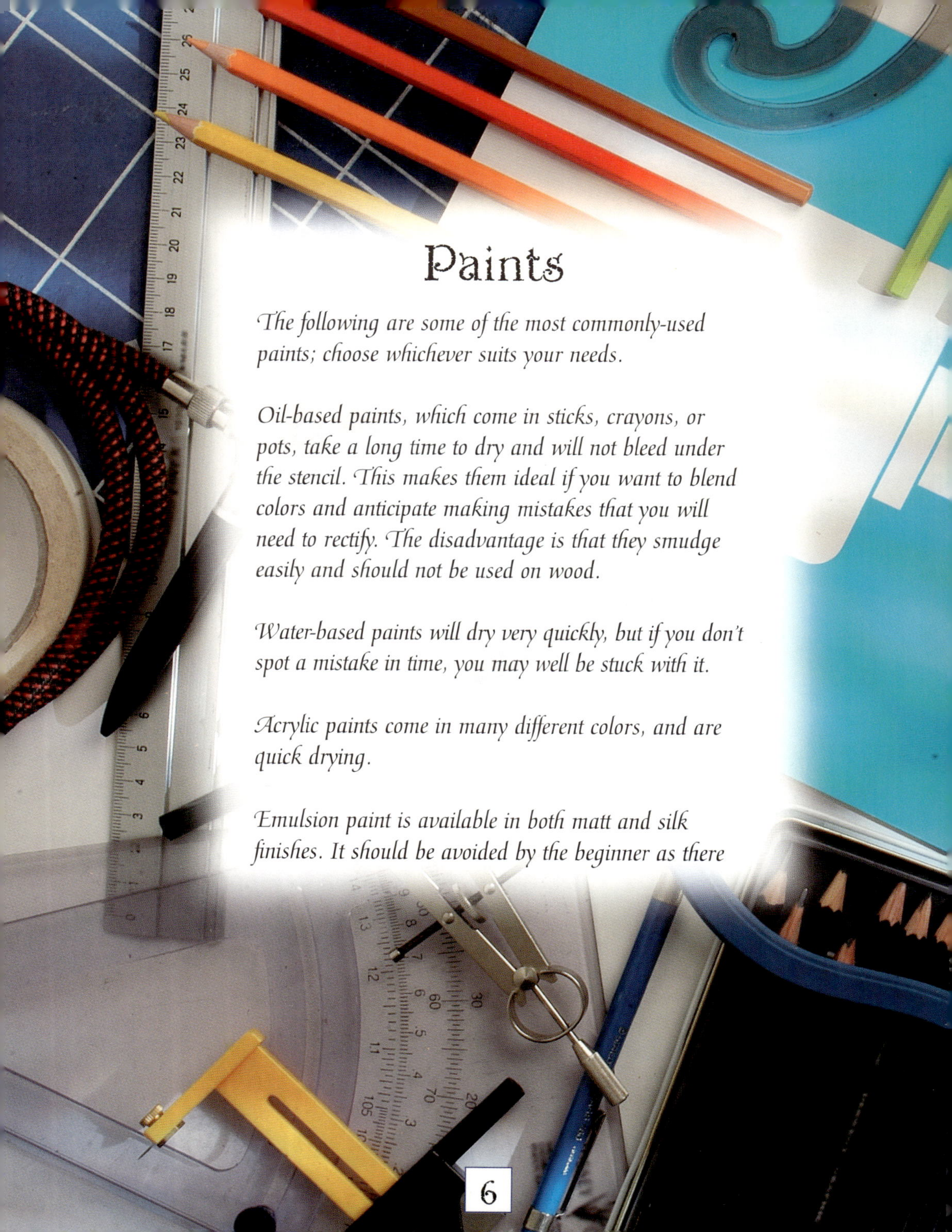

Paints

The following are some of the most commonly-used paints; choose whichever suits your needs.

Oil-based paints, which come in sticks, crayons, or pots, take a long time to dry and will not bleed under the stencil. This makes them ideal if you want to blend colors and anticipate making mistakes that you will need to rectify. The disadvantage is that they smudge easily and should not be used on wood.

Water-based paints will dry very quickly, but if you don't spot a mistake in time, you may well be stuck with it.

Acrylic paints come in many different colors, and are quick drying.

Emulsion paint is available in both matt and silk finishes. It should be avoided by the beginner as there

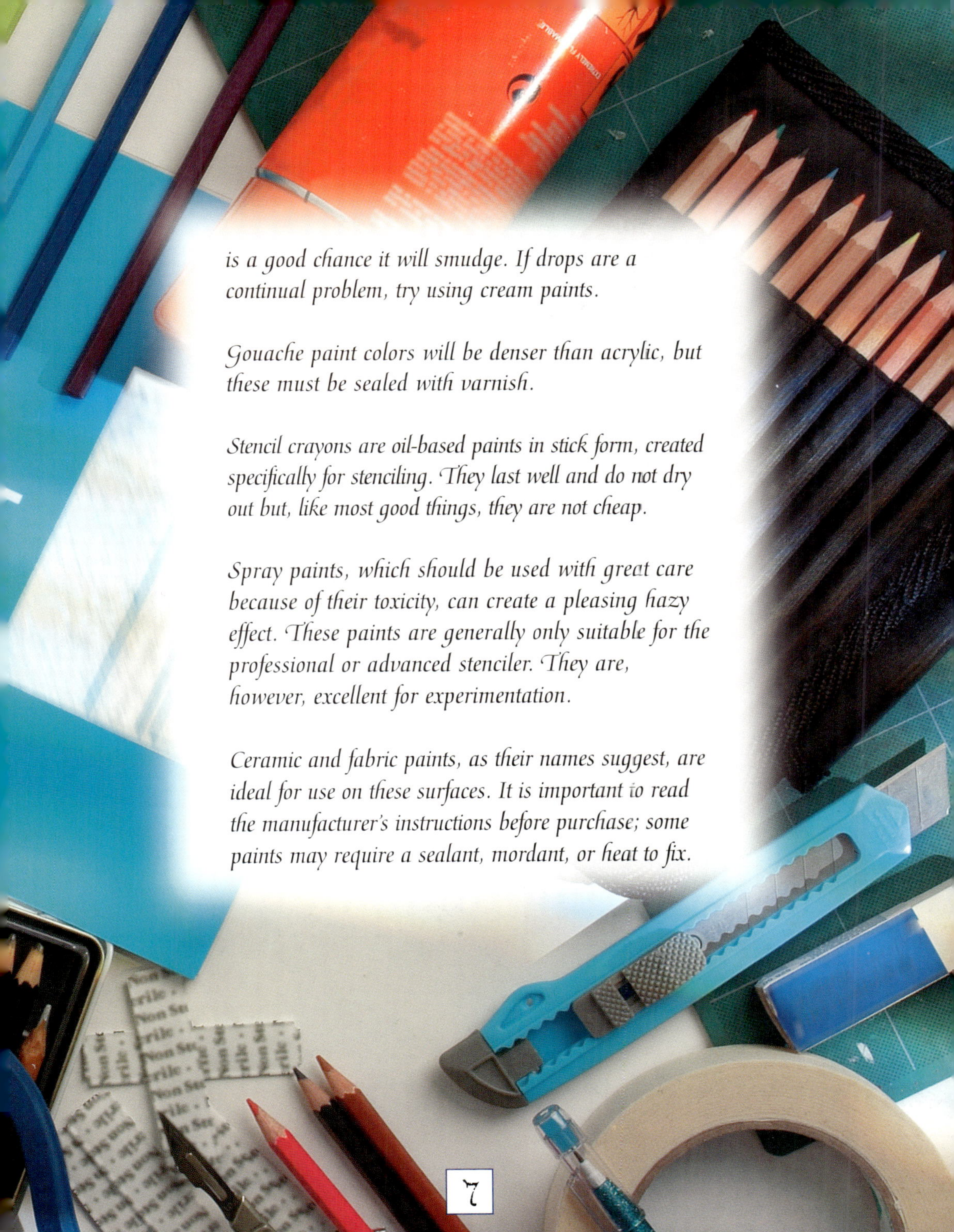

is a good chance it will smudge. If drops are a continual problem, try using cream paints.

Gouache paint colors will be denser than acrylic, but these must be sealed with varnish.

Stencil crayons are oil-based paints in stick form, created specifically for stenciling. They last well and do not dry out but, like most good things, they are not cheap.

Spray paints, which should be used with great care because of their toxicity, can create a pleasing hazy effect. These paints are generally only suitable for the professional or advanced stenciler. They are, however, excellent for experimentation.

Ceramic and fabric paints, as their names suggest, are ideal for use on these surfaces. It is important to read the manufacturer's instructions before purchase; some paints may require a sealant, mordant, or heat to fix.

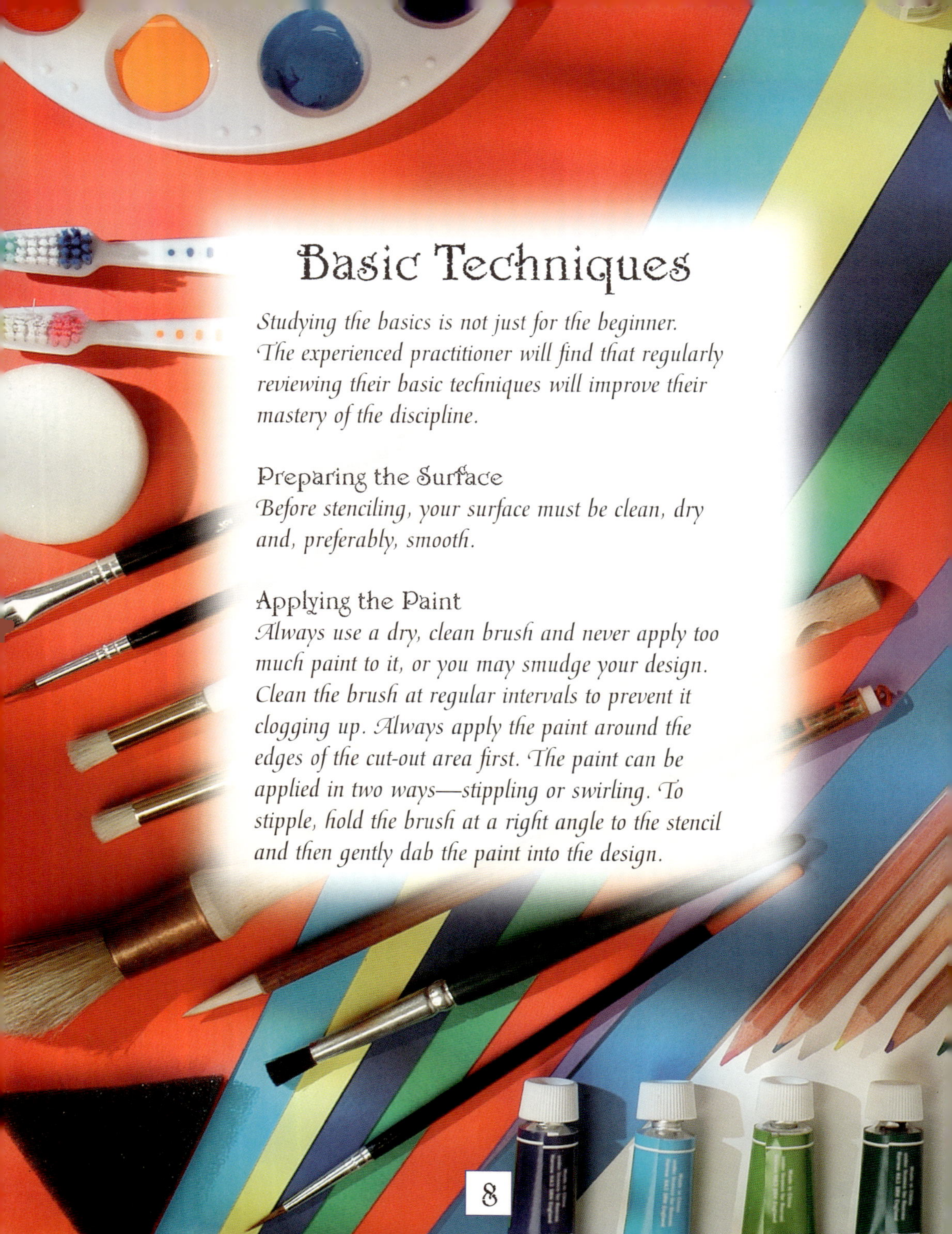

Basic Techniques

Studying the basics is not just for the beginner. The experienced practitioner will find that regularly reviewing their basic techniques will improve their mastery of the discipline.

Preparing the Surface

Before stenciling, your surface must be clean, dry and, preferably, smooth.

Applying the Paint

Always use a dry, clean brush and never apply too much paint to it, or you may smudge your design. Clean the brush at regular intervals to prevent it clogging up. Always apply the paint around the edges of the cut-out area first. The paint can be applied in two ways—stippling or swirling. To stipple, hold the brush at a right angle to the stencil and then gently dab the paint into the design.

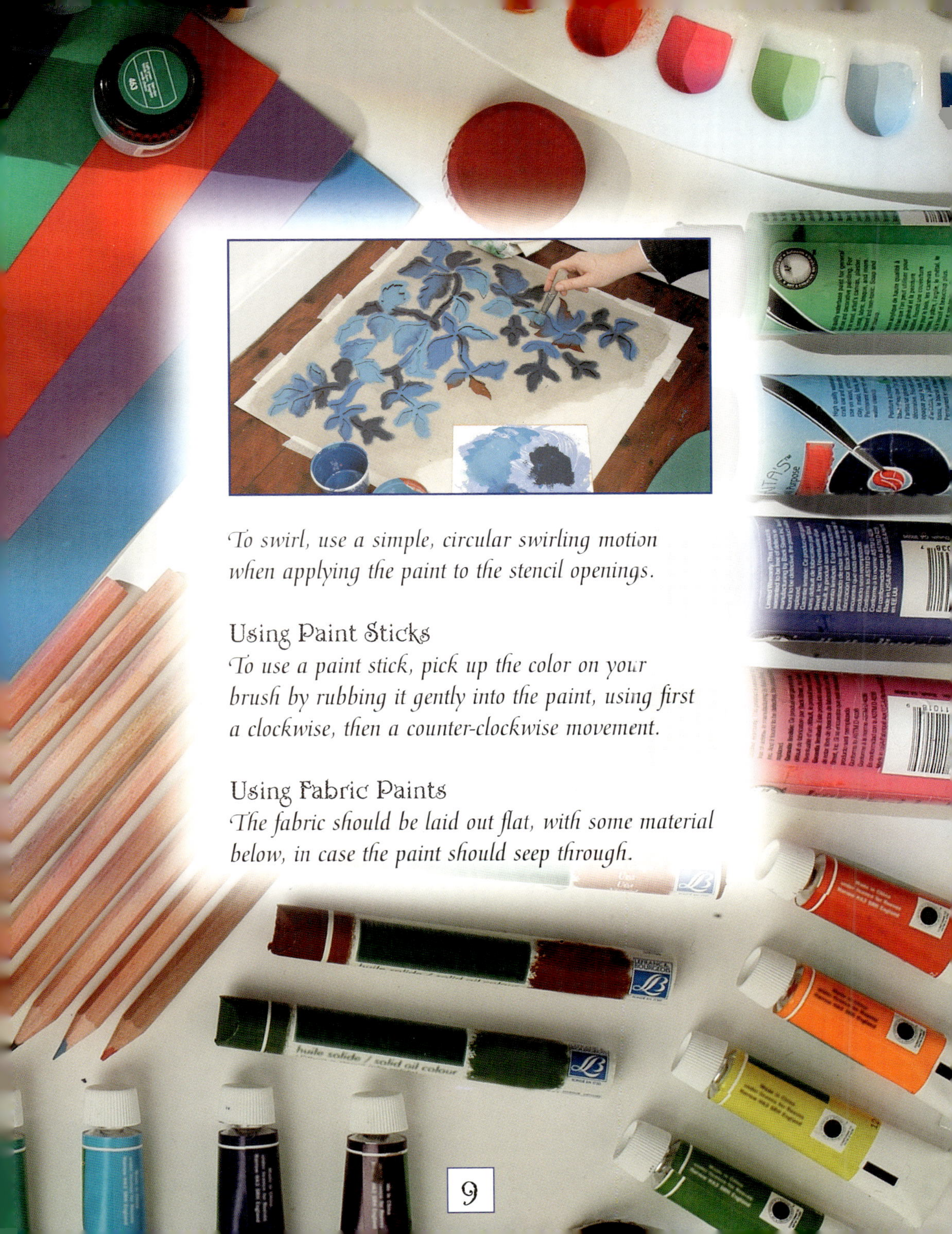

To swirl, use a simple, circular swirling motion when applying the paint to the stencil openings.

Using Paint Sticks

To use a paint stick, pick up the color on your brush by rubbing it gently into the paint, using first a clockwise, then a counter-clockwise movement.

Using Fabric Paints

The fabric should be laid out flat, with some material below, in case the paint should seep through.

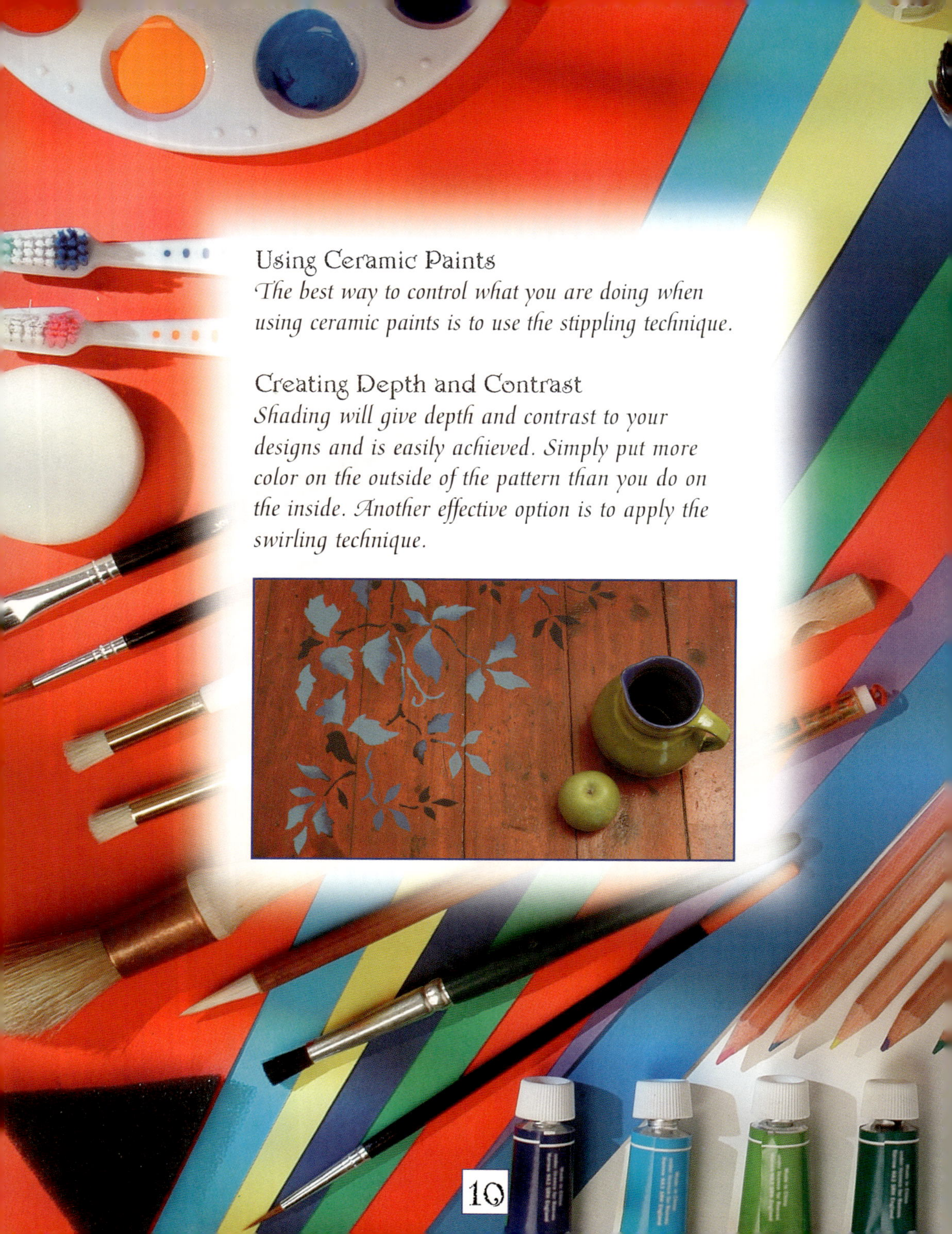

Using Ceramic Paints

The best way to control what you are doing when using ceramic paints is to use the stippling technique.

Creating Depth and Contrast

Shading will give depth and contrast to your designs and is easily achieved. Simply put more color on the outside of the pattern than you do on the inside. Another effective option is to apply the swirling technique.

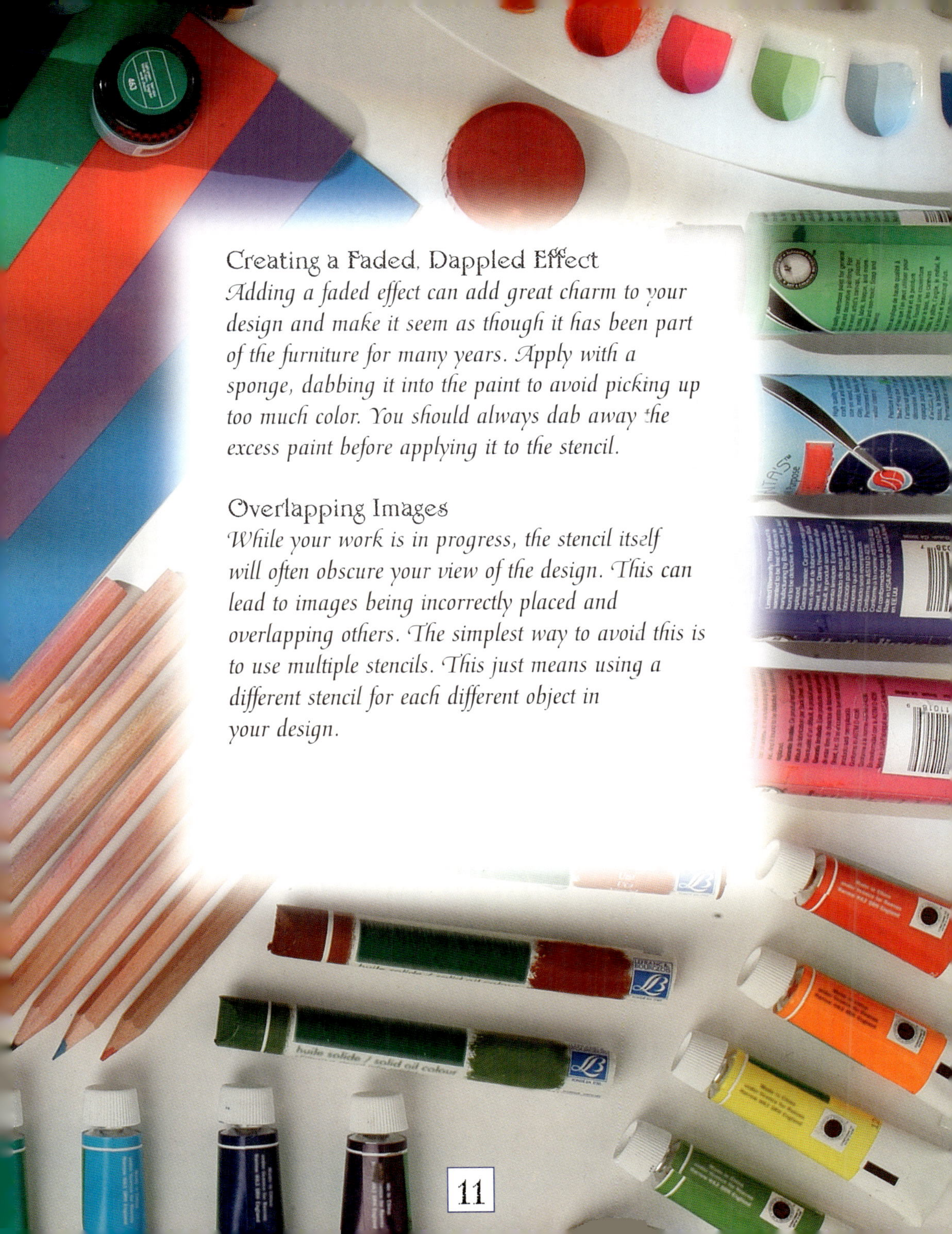

Creating a Faded, Dappled Effect

Adding a faded effect can add great charm to your design and make it seem as though it has been part of the furniture for many years. Apply with a sponge, dabbing it into the paint to avoid picking up too much color. You should always dab away the excess paint before applying it to the stencil.

Overlapping Images

While your work is in progress, the stencil itself will often obscure your view of the design. This can lead to images being incorrectly placed and overlapping others. The simplest way to avoid this is to use multiple stencils. This just means using a different stencil for each different object in your design.

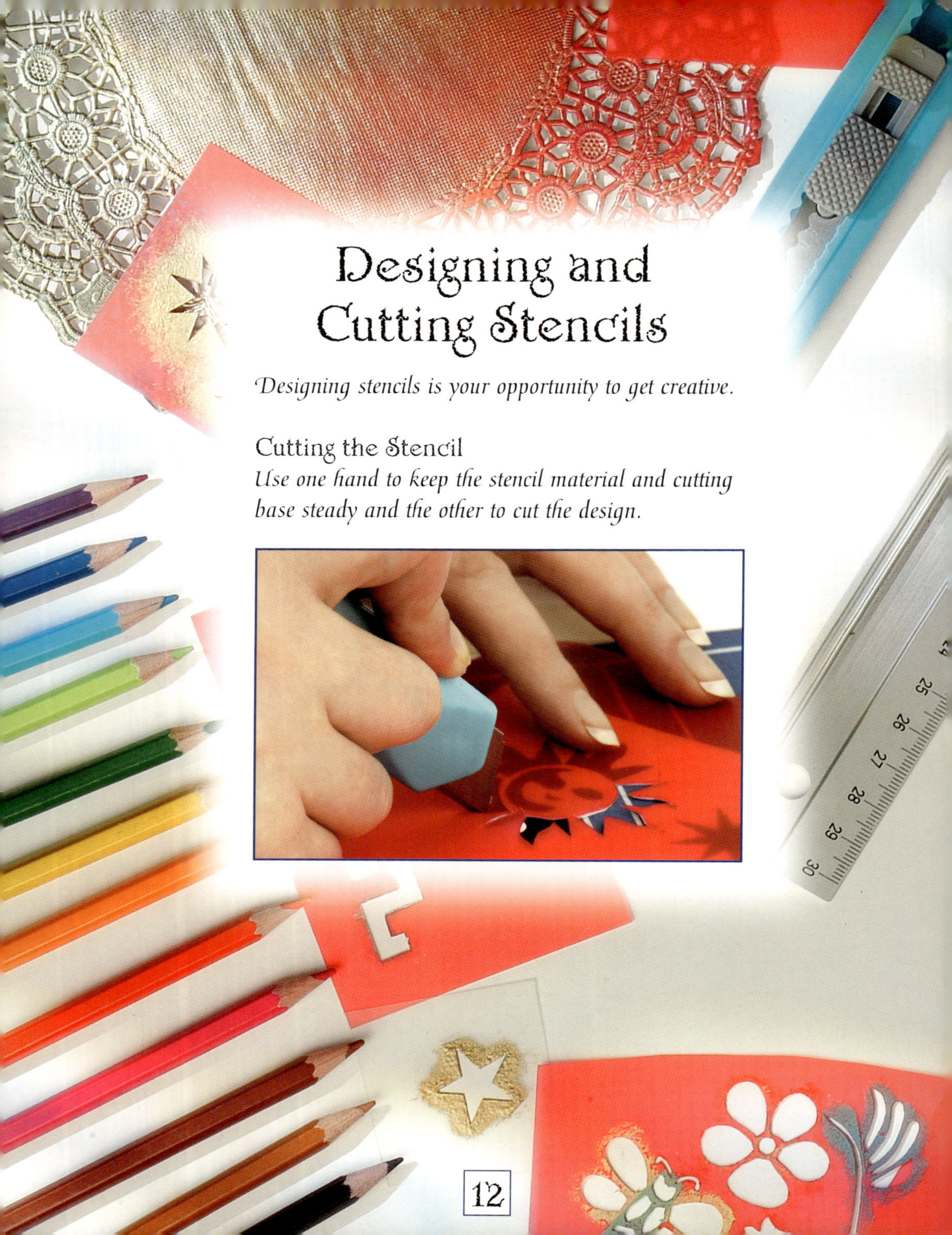

Designing and Cutting Stencils

Designing stencils is your opportunity to get creative.

Cutting the Stencil

Use one hand to keep the stencil material and cutting base steady and the other to cut the design.

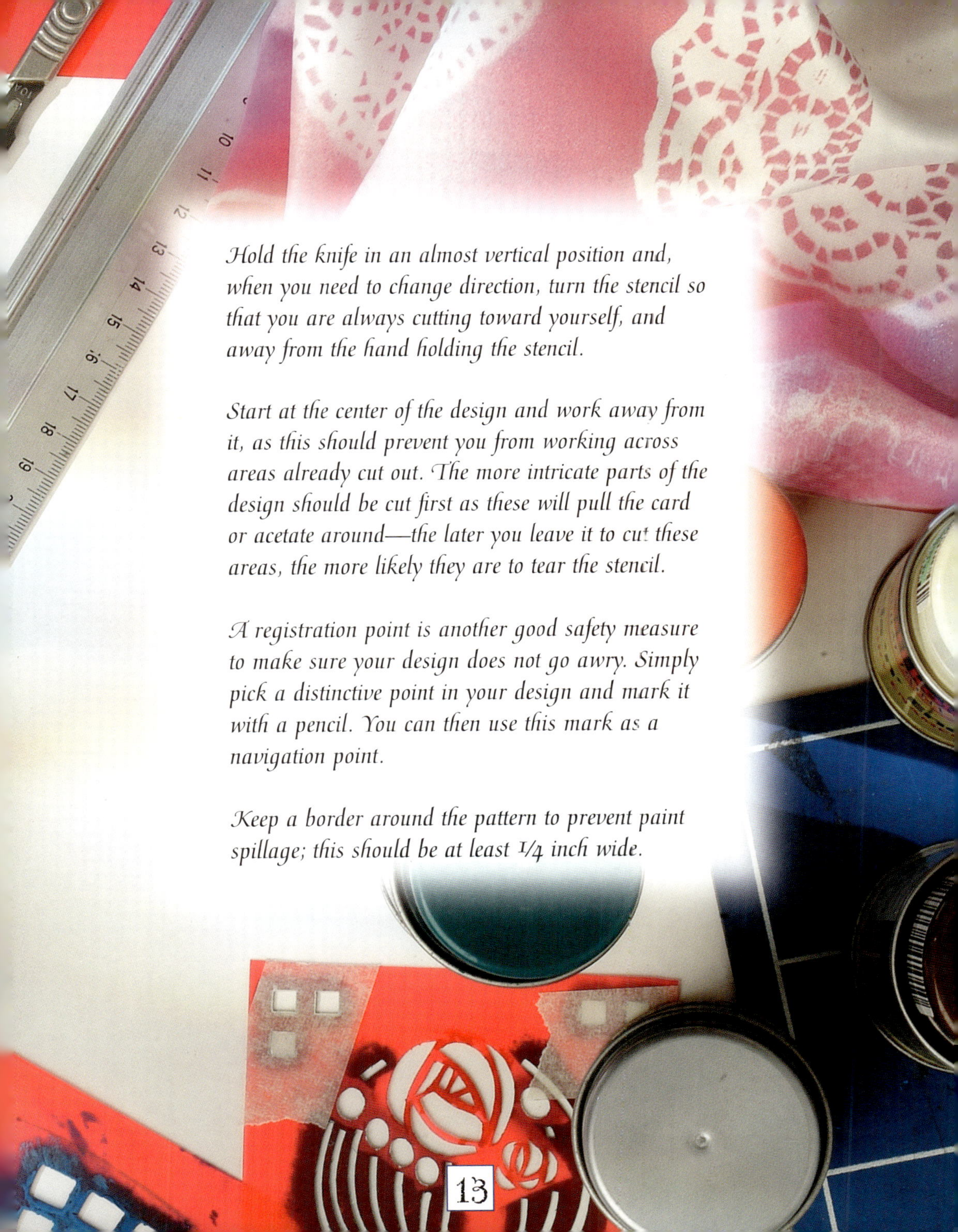

Hold the knife in an almost vertical position and, when you need to change direction, turn the stencil so that you are always cutting toward yourself, and away from the hand holding the stencil.

Start at the center of the design and work away from it, as this should prevent you from working across areas already cut out. The more intricate parts of the design should be cut first as these will pull the card or acetate around—the later you leave it to cut these areas, the more likely they are to tear the stencil.

A registration point is another good safety measure to make sure your design does not go awry. Simply pick a distinctive point in your design and mark it with a pencil. You can then use this mark as a navigation point.

Keep a border around the pattern to prevent paint spillage; this should be at least 1/4 inch wide.

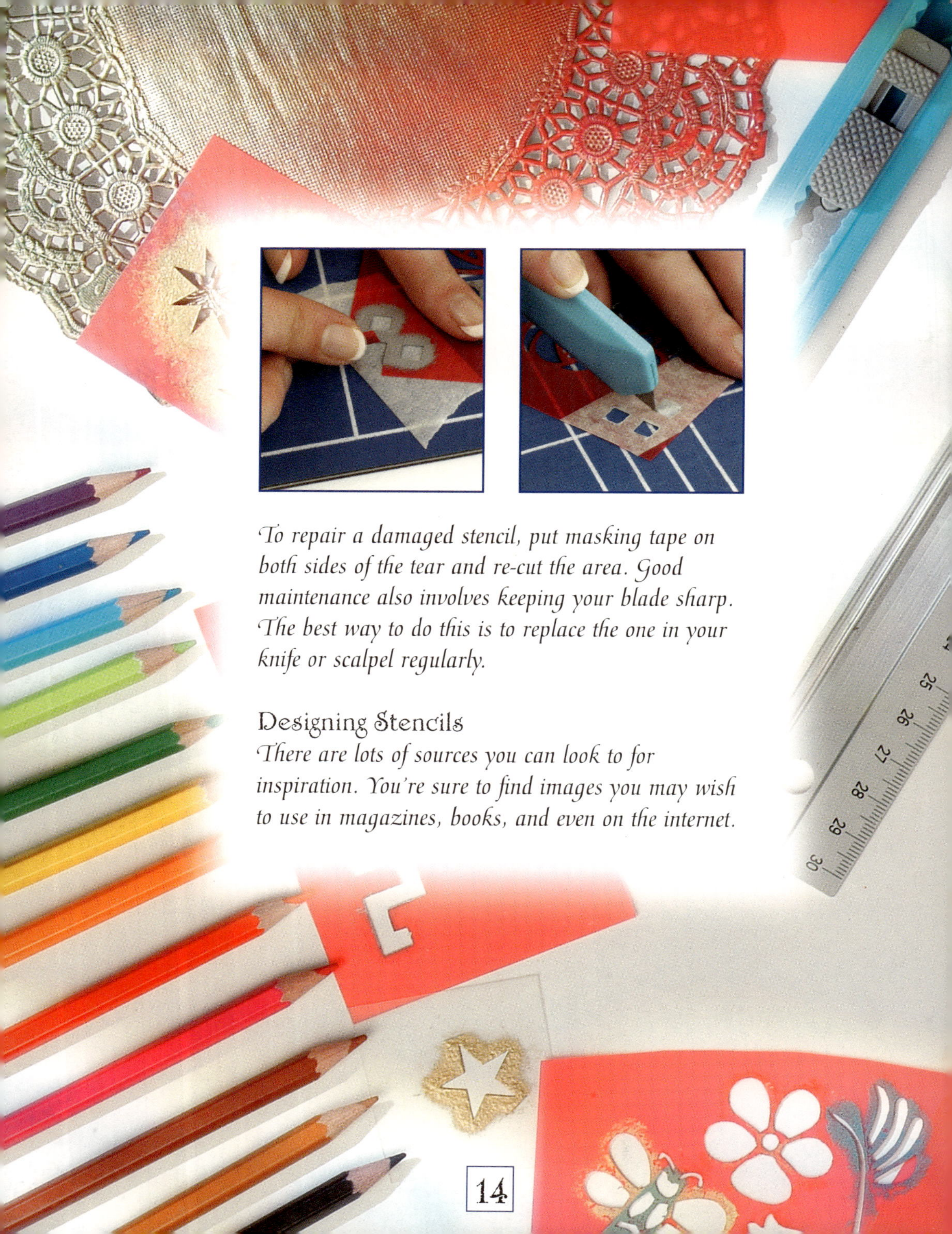

To repair a damaged stencil, put masking tape on both sides of the tear and re-cut the area. Good maintenance also involves keeping your blade sharp. The best way to do this is to replace the one in your knife or scalpel regularly.

Designing Stencils

There are lots of sources you can look to for inspiration. You're sure to find images you may wish to use in magazines, books, and even on the internet.

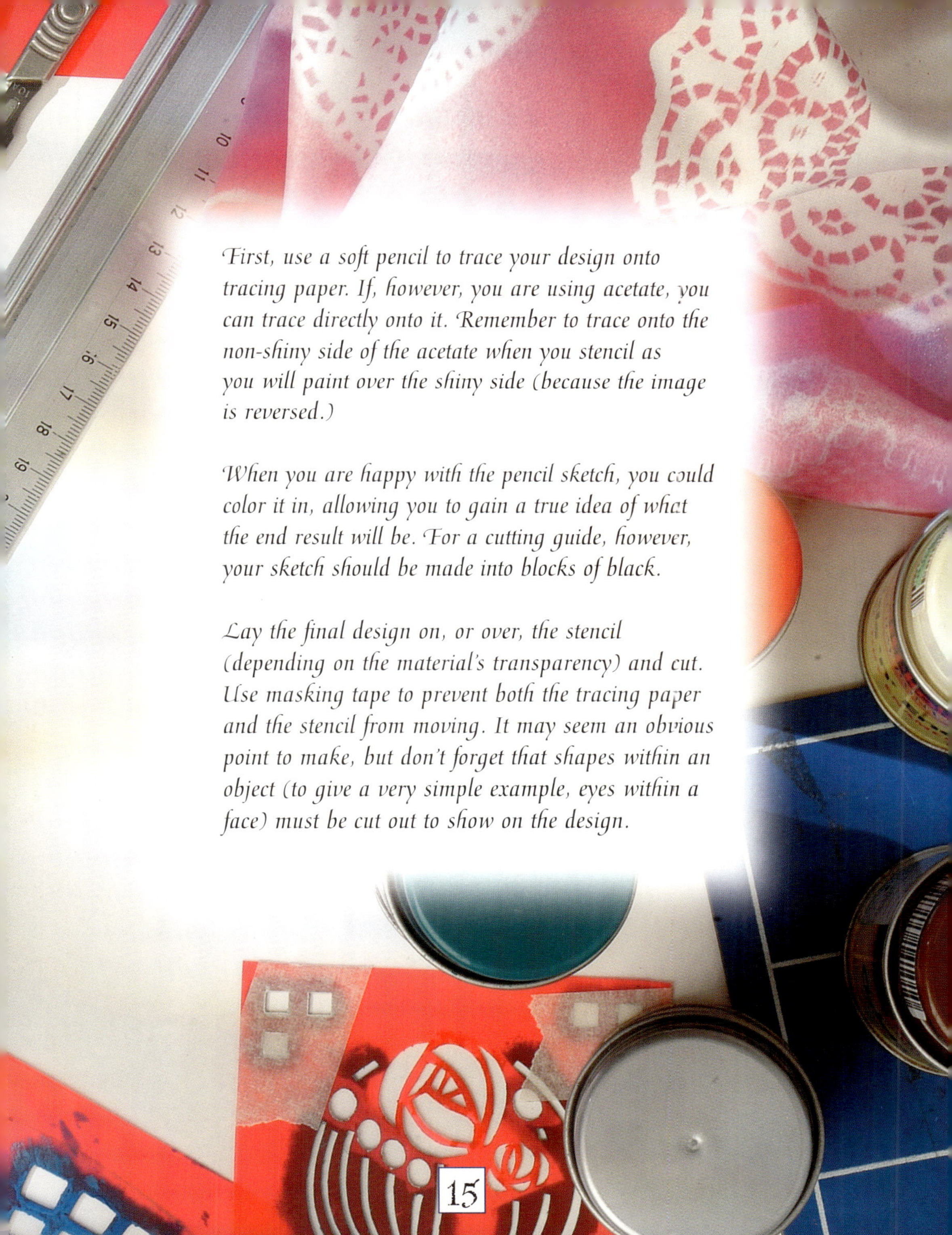

First, use a soft pencil to trace your design onto tracing paper. If, however, you are using acetate, you can trace directly onto it. Remember to trace onto the non-shiny side of the acetate when you stencil as you will paint over the shiny side (because the image is reversed.)

When you are happy with the pencil sketch, you could color it in, allowing you to gain a true idea of what the end result will be. For a cutting guide, however, your sketch should be made into blocks of black.

Lay the final design on, or over, the stencil (depending on the material's transparency) and cut. Use masking tape to prevent both the tracing paper and the stencil from moving. It may seem an obvious point to make, but don't forget that shapes within an object (to give a very simple example, eyes within a face) must be cut out to show on the design.

Preparing a Wall

Preparation may seem a chore, but it is the key to a really effective wall design.

Although walls do not need to be perfectly smooth, all traces of wallpaper should be removed, and significant indentations filled in. If you want to stencil onto bare plaster, you should treat it with a universal sealant first.

Corners

It is unlikely that a repeated design will fit perfectly to the length of your wall. You can hide this by subtly varying the length of the gaps between each repetition. If this is done well, the eye will not notice. Alternatively, you can use a different design at either end of the wall to act as "bookends" for the main feature. Another option, and one that has a certain organic appeal, is to take elements from the original design and combine them into a corner motif.

Lining up

When you have decided the approximate height at which you want your design, use a level and ruler to mark, at points along the surface, a true line. Mark where the center point of your design will be by pinning pieces of string from one corner to another. The center point will be where the pieces of string cross. Should you deem it necessary to establish the true height of the wall, you will need to use a weighted plumb line.

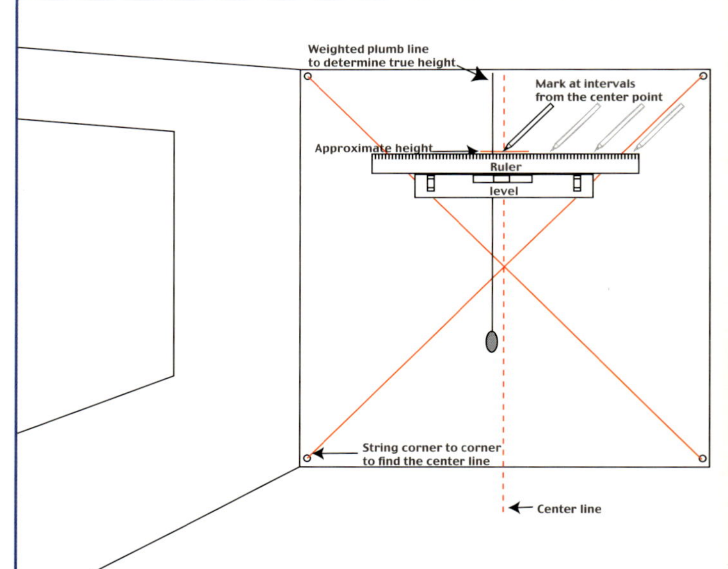

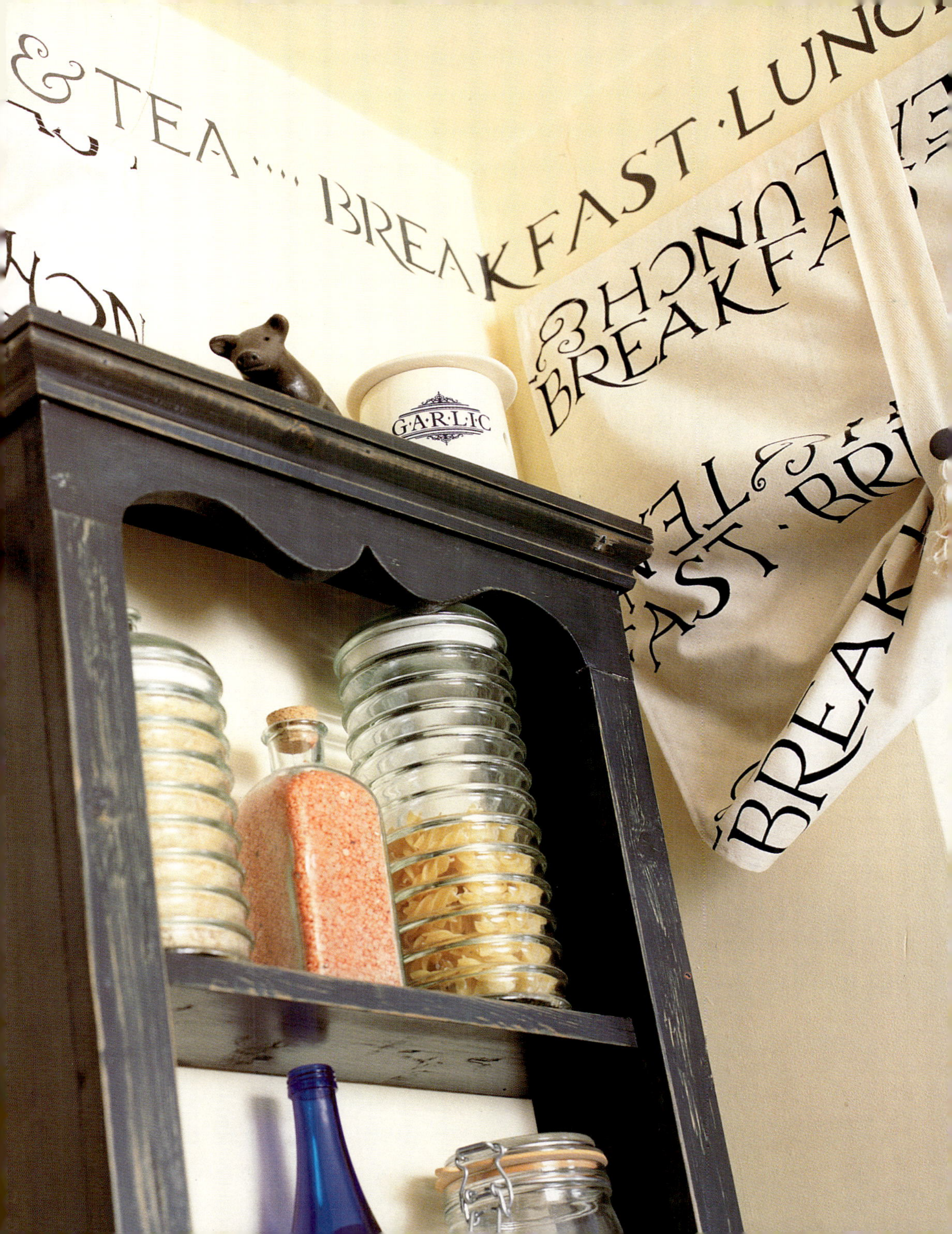
& TEA .... BREAKFAST
G·A·R·L·I·C

Time for Drinks

Add a bit of extra glamor to your party or dining room with these glitzy cocktail display glasses. Stars are one of the simplest designs to apply to glass, but why not try butterflies or flowers once you've mastered this project?

YOU WILL NEED:

- *two large cocktail glasses*
- *gold, acrylic craft paint*
- *masking tape*
- *stencil card*
- *a craft knife*
- *a pencil*
- *a stencil brush*
- *a fine paintbrush*
- *a paper towel*
- *a saucer for paint*
- *gloss acrylic varnish*
- *a brush for varnishing*

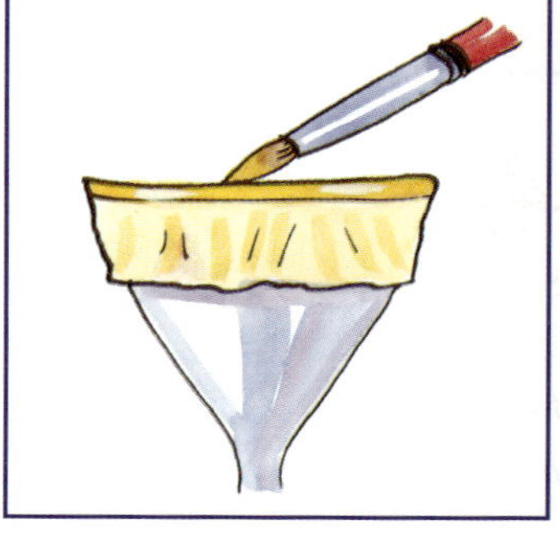

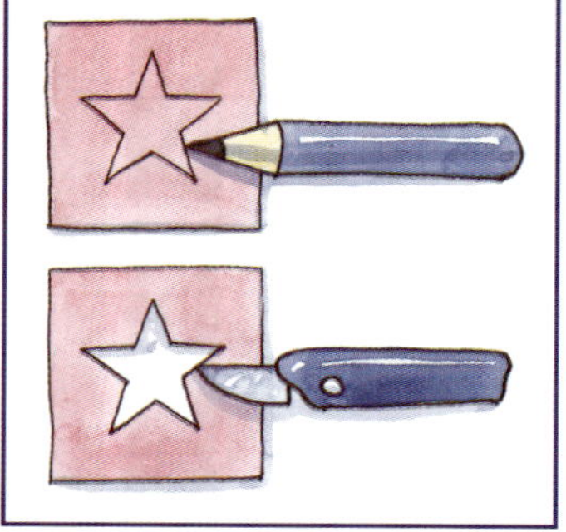

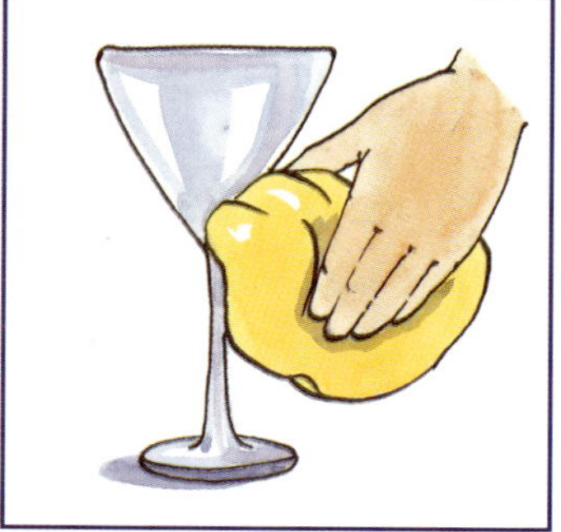

1 *To make the stencil for this design, trace over the template on page 20 onto stencil card, and carefully cut it out using a craft knife.*

2 *Wash your cocktail glasses in warm, soapy water, and dry them thoroughly.*

3 *Leaving a gap of about 1/8 inch from the top of the glass, wrap a length of masking tape around the rim. Fill in this area with gold paint using a fine paintbrush. Allow this strip to dry completely, then apply a second coat. When the second coat has dried, carefully remove the masking tape.*

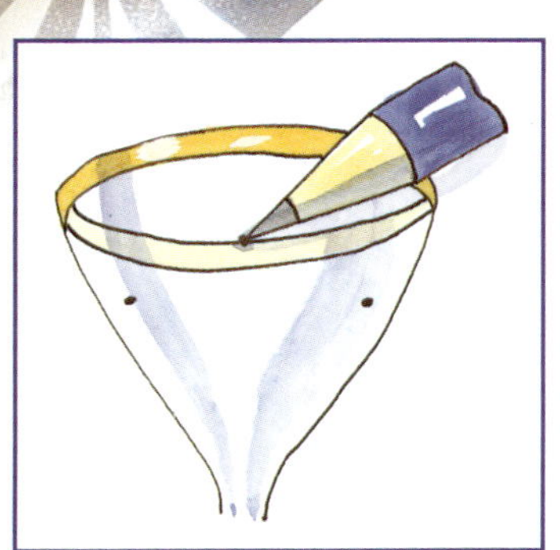

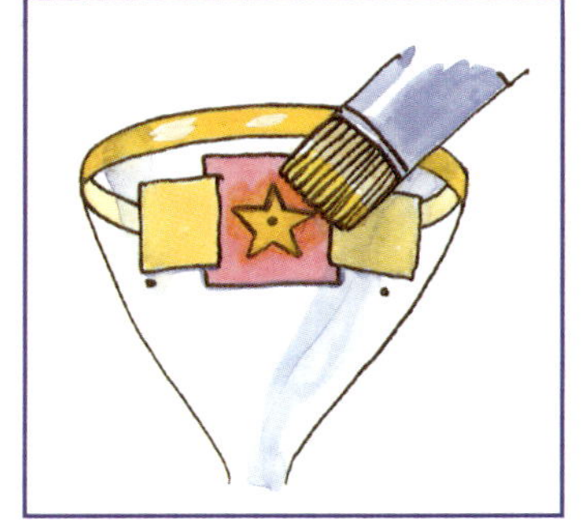

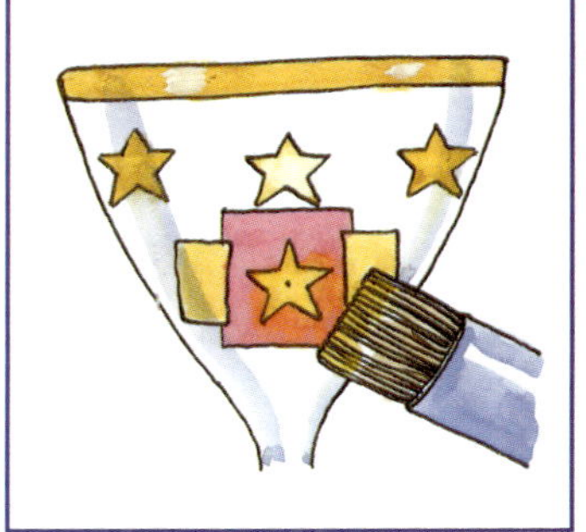

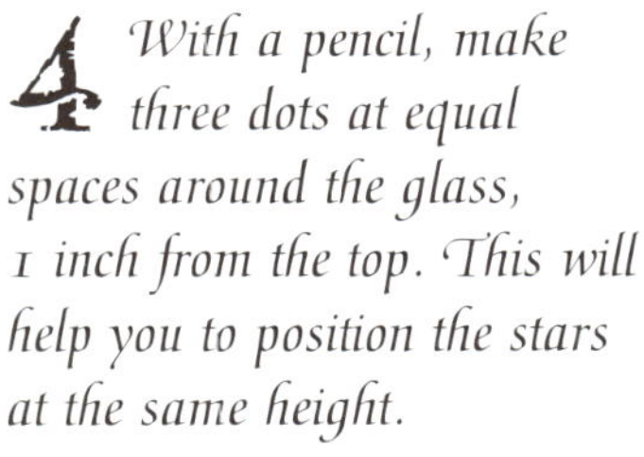

4 With a pencil, make three dots at equal spaces around the glass, 1 inch from the top. This will help you to position the stars at the same height.

Tip: Don't worry if your design bleeds a little, as you can always tidy up the edges with a toothpick when it is dry. Simply use the tip to carefully scrape away the paint.

5 Place the stencil over the center of one of the dots and secure it with masking tape. Dip your stencil brush into gold paint, dab off the excess onto a paper towel, and apply the paint to the stencil. Once finished, remove the stencil carefully so as not to smudge the paint. Repeat this for the other two remaining dots and leave to dry.

6 Now make three more dots halfway between each of your first dots, but this time make them 2 inches down from the top of the glass. Place the stencil over the center of one of the dots and secure with masking tape. Dip your stencil brush into gold paint, dab off the excess onto a paper towel, and apply the paint to the stencil. Once finished, remove the stencil carefully, and allow to dry. Repeat with the two remaining dots and leave to dry.

Tip: Instead of acrylic paint, you could use special glass paint available from craft stores.

• You don't have to stop here—continue your design on other table or decorative items. Why not try adding stenciled napkins or place settings? You could also take the glasses one step further by adding a little glitter paint for extra sparkle around the rim or in the center of the stars.

Warning: Whichever paint you opt for, these glasses should only be used as decorative ornaments and not as drinking vessels.

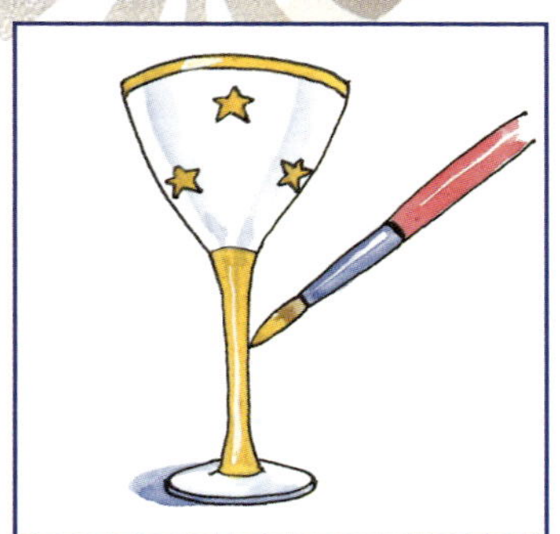

7 *Using a paintbrush and gold paint, cover the stem of the glass, but leave the base clear of paint. Allow this to dry, then apply a second coat.*

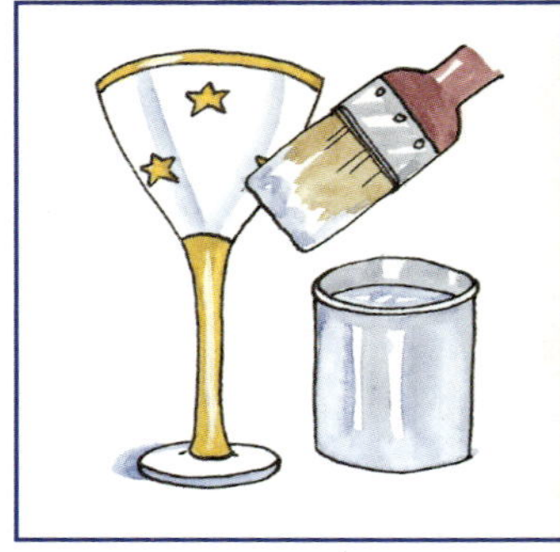

8 *Leave all the paint to dry completely, then apply a coat of gloss acrylic varnish over the entire outside of your finished glass. Repeat the entire design on the second cocktail glass.*

TEMPLATE AND COLOR GUIDE

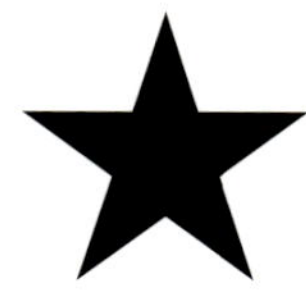

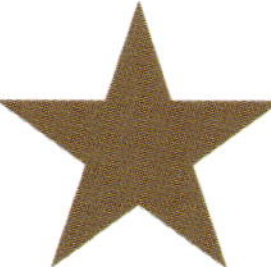

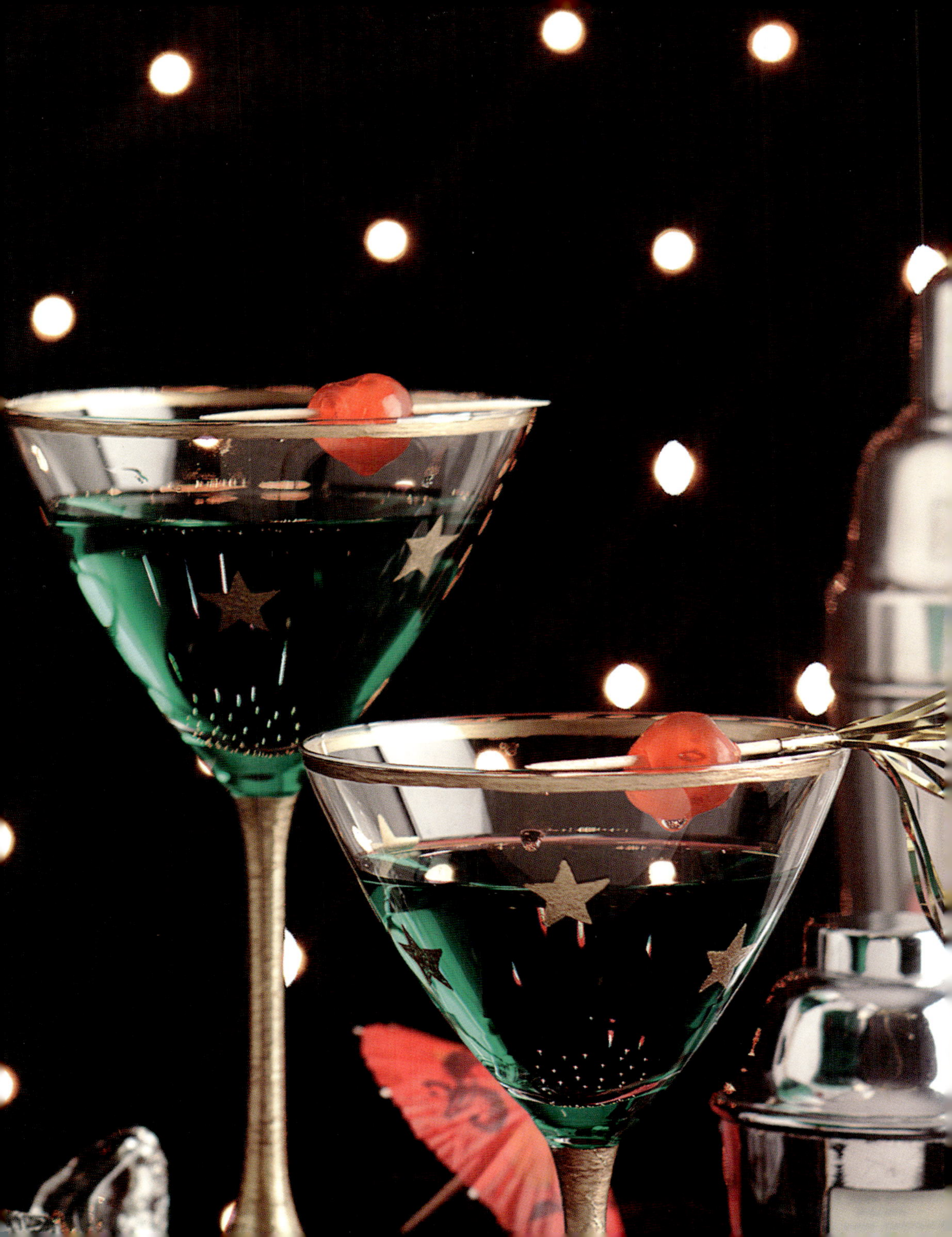

At your Service

Stenciling needn't be all about flowers and swirls; keep it clean and simple with geometric designs and experiment with color effects, as shown with this plate and bowl.

YOU WILL NEED:

- *a large plain plate and bowl*
- *blue and white acrylic craft paint, or ceramic paint*
- *masking tape*
- *stencil card*
- *a pencil*
- *a ruler*
- *a craft knife*
- *a stencil brush*
- *paper towels*
- *a saucer for paint*
- *gloss acrylic varnish*
- *a brush for varnishing*

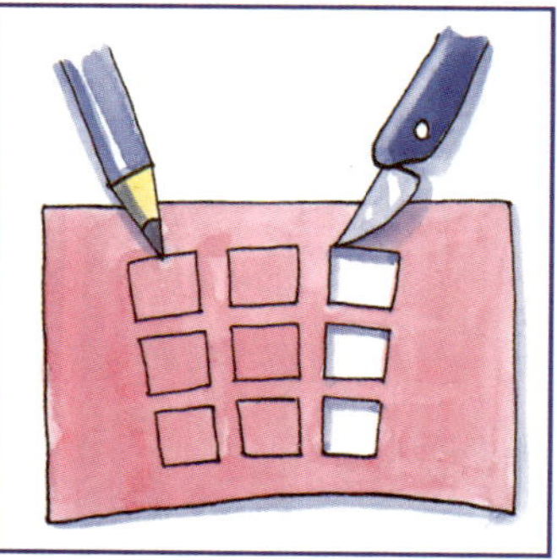

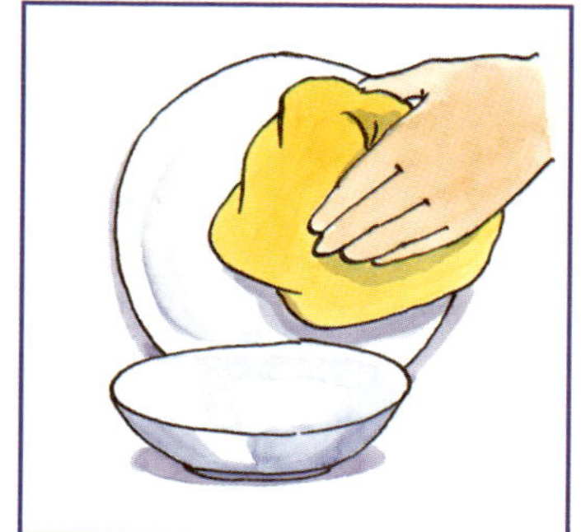

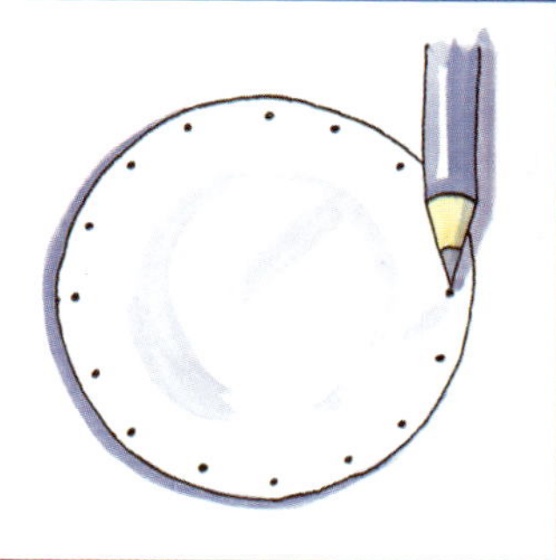

1 *To make the stencil for this design, trace over the template on page 24 onto stencil card, and carefully cut it out using a craft knife.*

2 *Wipe your plate and bowl free of dust and dirt using a damp cloth and dry thoroughly.*

For the plate design:

3 *With a pencil, make dots at equal distances around the edge of the plate so that the plate is divided into sixteen equal sections.*

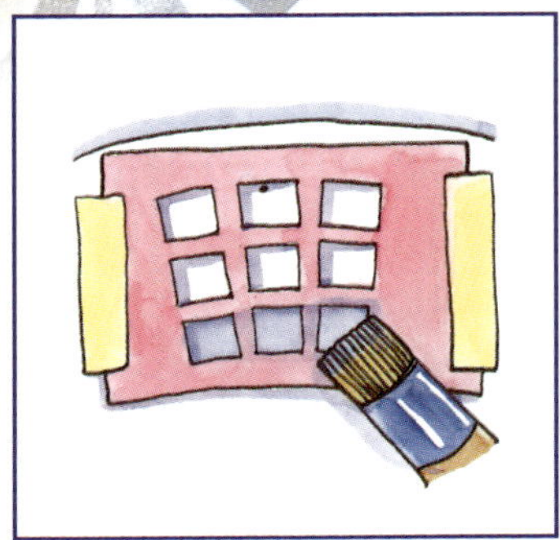

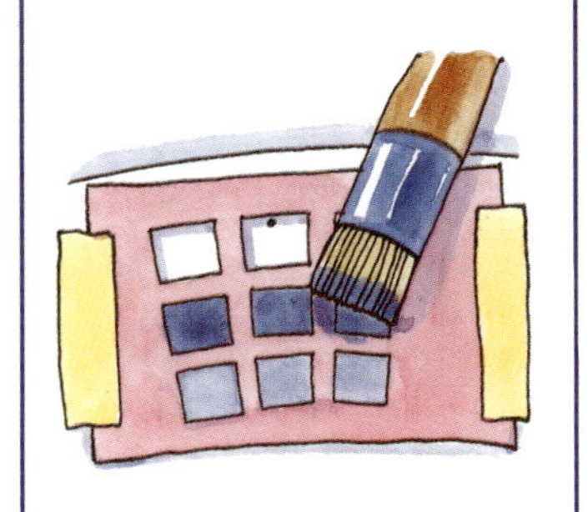

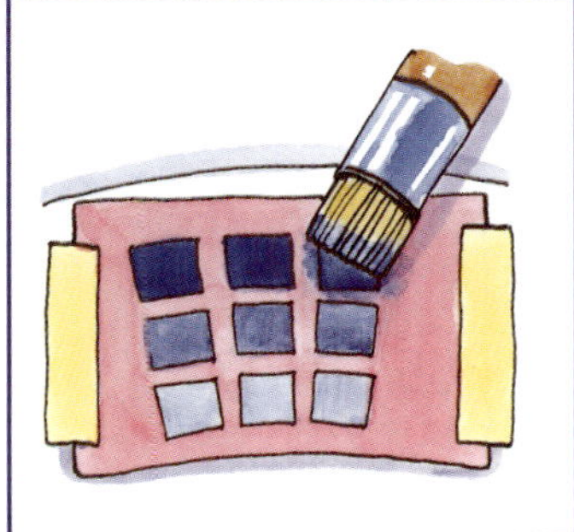

4 Place the stencil over the first pencil dot and secure with masking tape. On a saucer mix up three different shades of blue; a light blue, a mid blue, and a dark blue. Dip your stencil brush into the light blue paint, dab the excess onto a paper towel, and apply the paint to the bottom three squares on the stencil.

5 Rinse your brush thoroughly then dry it on a paper towel. Dip it into the mid blue color, then apply the paint to the middle three squares of your design.

Tip: You could use three brushes, one for each color. This will speed up the process.

6 Rinse and dry your brush thoroughly, then apply the dark blue color to the top three squares of your design. Remove the stencil carefully, and allow to dry.

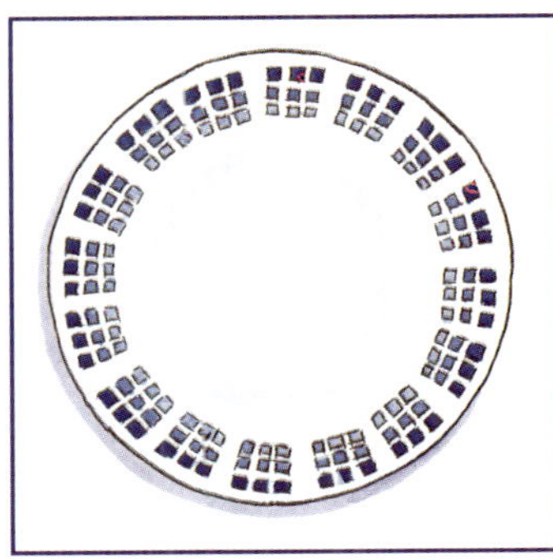

7 Repeat steps 4–6 in the other fifteen sections of the plate.

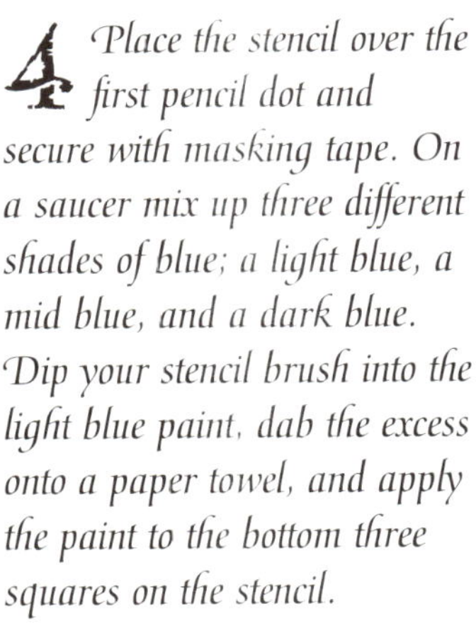

Tip: If you are finding it difficult to stencil straight onto the plate, apply a coat of acrylic varnish first. This will provide a base for your paint to stick to. Once again, this plate and bowl set are only suitable for decoration. Try using the plate as an underplate to set off your own china. Or why not complete a full service and display your efforts in a traditional dresser?

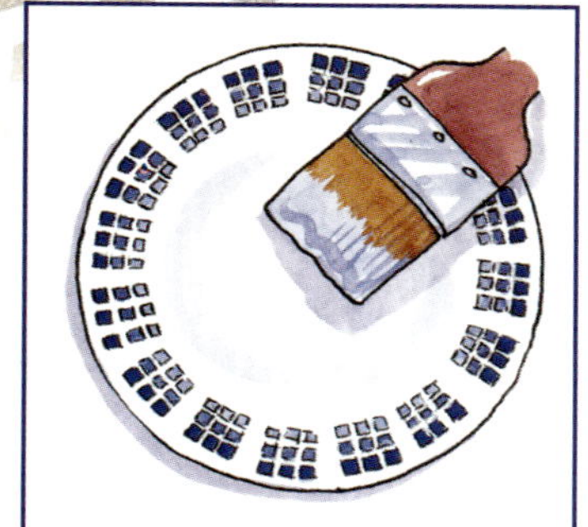

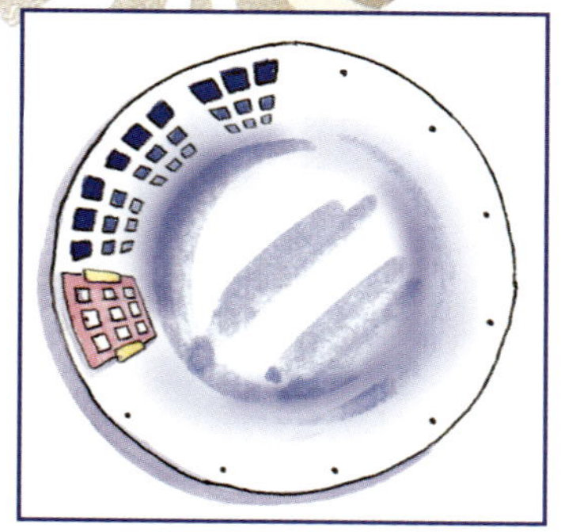

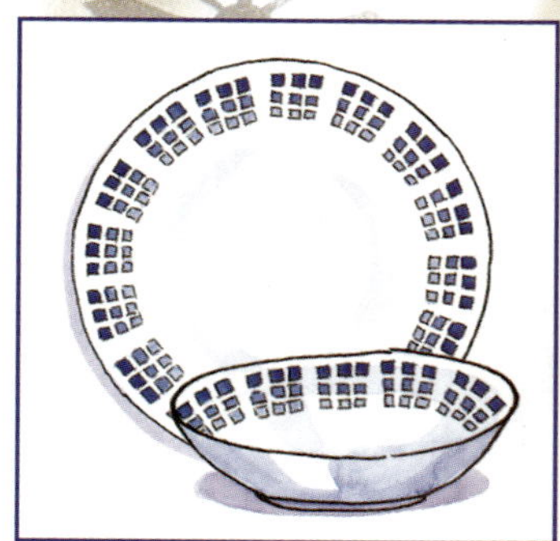

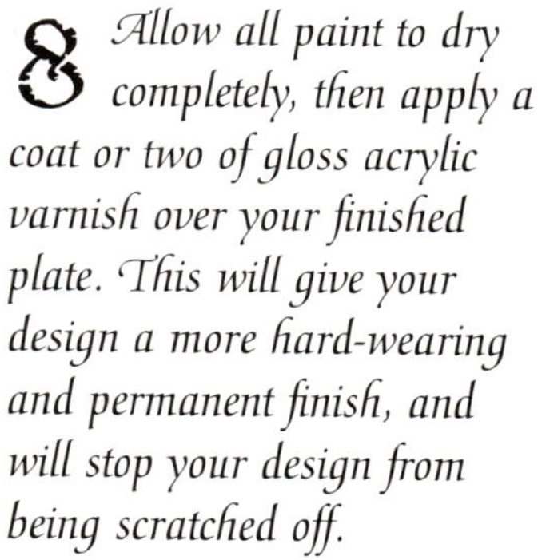

8 *Allow all paint to dry completely, then apply a coat or two of gloss acrylic varnish over your finished plate. This will give your design a more hard-wearing and permanent finish, and will stop your design from being scratched off.*

For the bowl design:

9 *With a pencil, make dots at equal distances around the edge of the bowl so that it is divided into twelve equal sections. Secure the stencil with masking tape, then follow the sequence of light blue, mid blue, and dark blue to form the stenciled design around the edge of the bowl. Repeat for every dot on the bowl. Allow all paint to dry completely, then apply two coats of gloss acrylic varnish over your finished bowl.*

TEMPLATE AND COLOR GUIDE

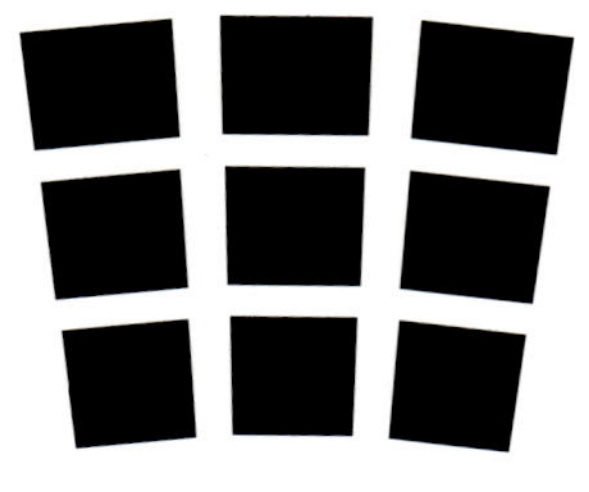

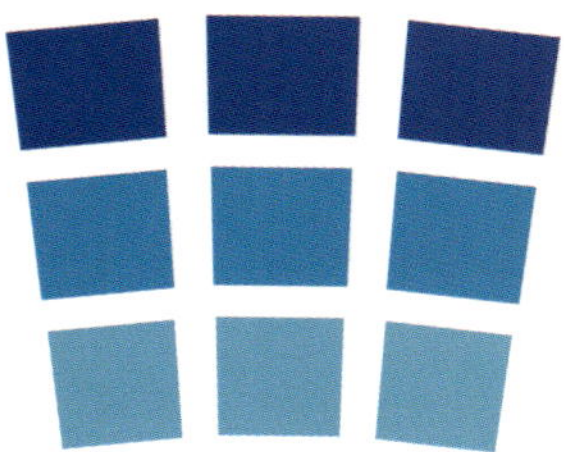

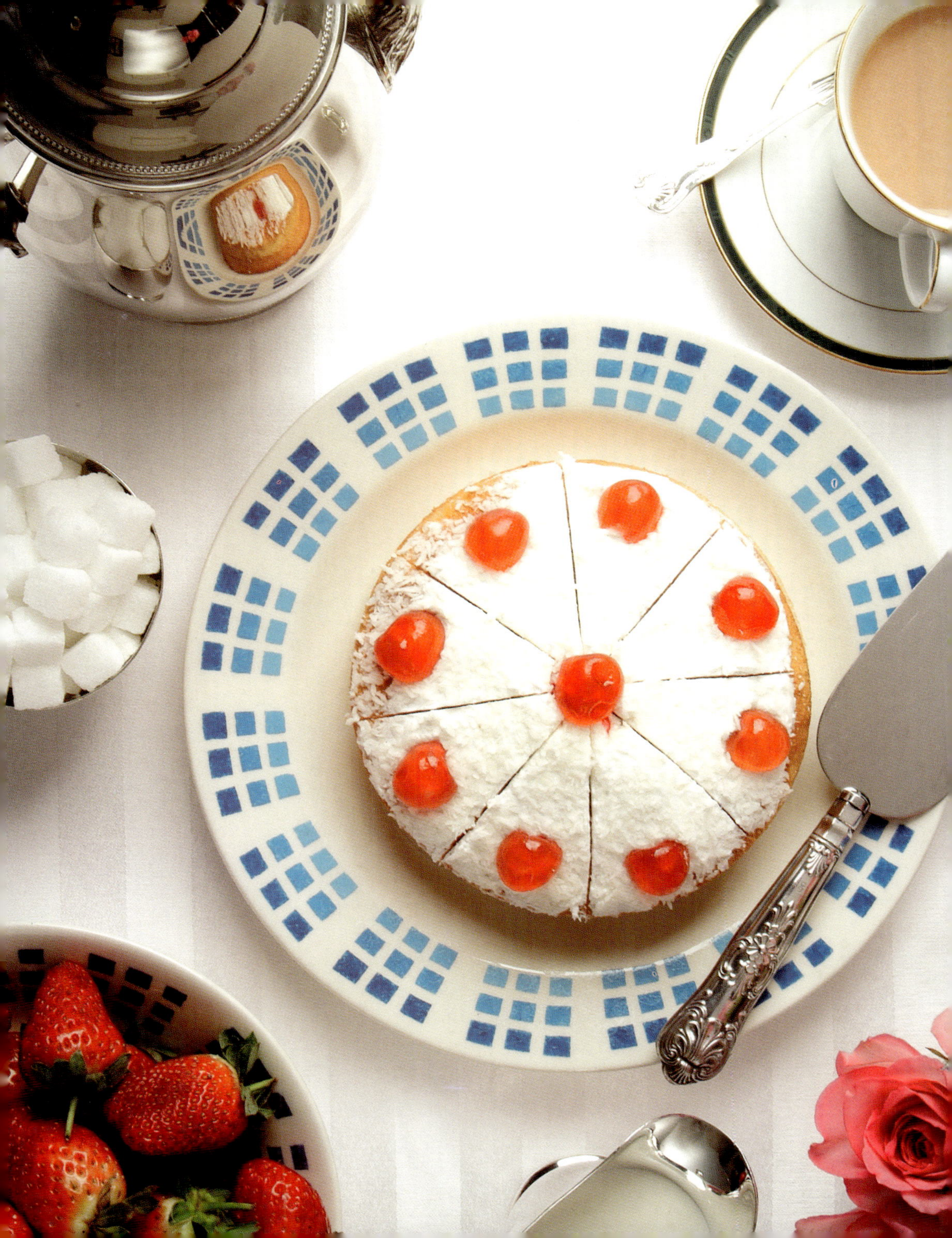

Doing More with Metal

Even everyday items need a lift sometimes and simple designs added to metal items like salt and pepper pots can really make a difference.

YOU WILL NEED:

- *metal salt and pepper pots*
- *white and silver acrylic craft paint*
- *stencil card*
- *a pencil*
- *a craft knife*
- *masking tape*
- *a stencil brush*
- *a paper towel*
- *a saucer for paint*
- *gloss acrylic varnish*
- *a brush for varnishing*

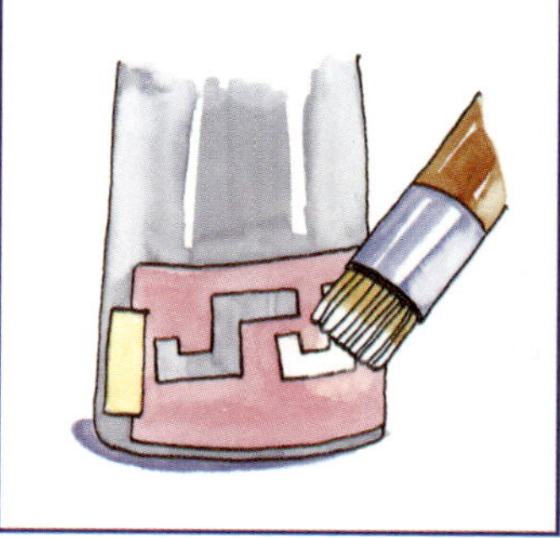

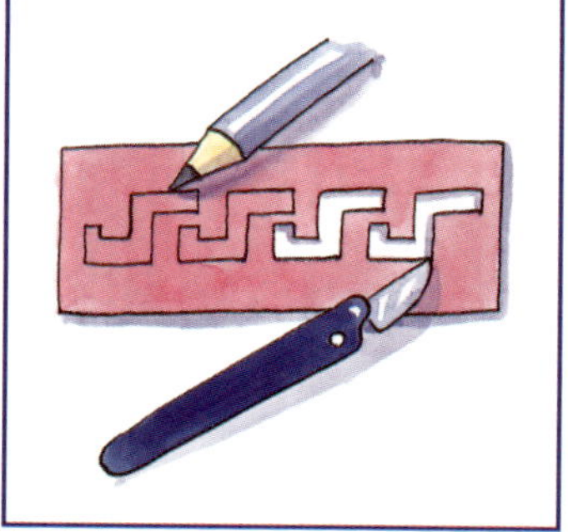

1 *To make the stencil for this design, trace over the template on page 28 onto stencil card, and carefully cut it out using a craft knife.*

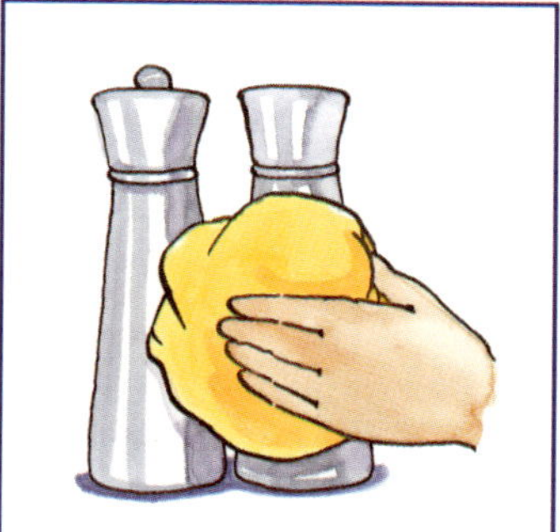

2 *Clean, and preferably empty, the salt and pepper pots, and ensure they are completely dry before you begin.*

3 *Place your stencil onto the pepper pot about 1/2 inch from the bottom edge, and secure with masking tape. Dip your stencil brush into white paint, dab the excess onto a paper towel, and apply the paint to the stencil. Once finished, remove the stencil carefully, so as not to smudge the paint, and allow to dry.*

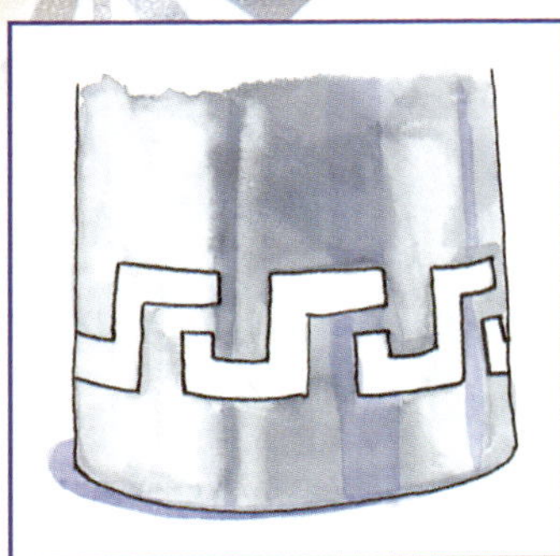

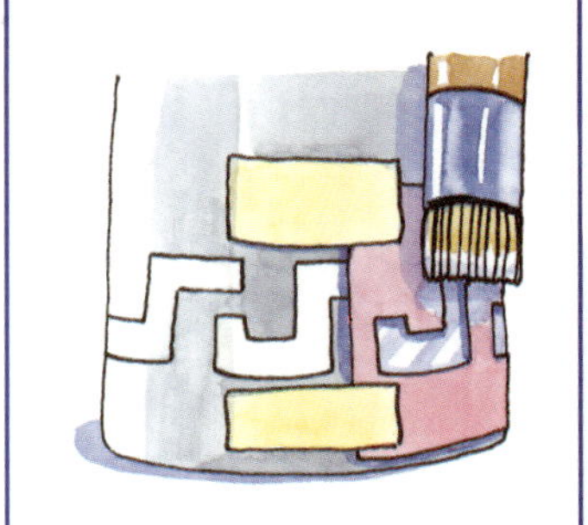

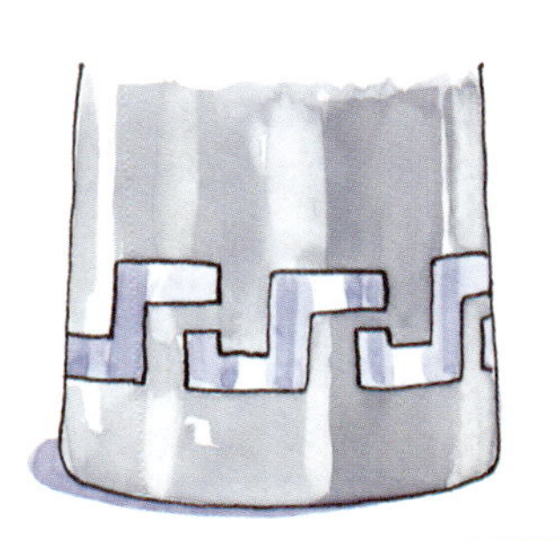

4 Move the stencil around the pepper pot and repeat step 3 to continue the design around the entire bottom edge. Leave until completely dry.

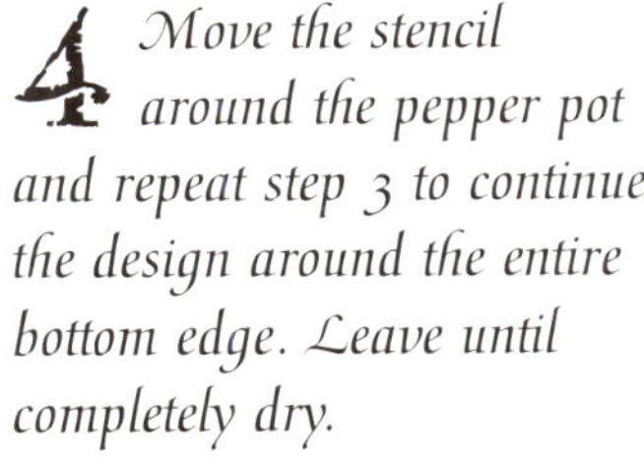

Tip: To avoid having to reposition the stencil, measure the circumference of the pots, and create a long, thin stencil which can be wrapped all the way around the pot. Make sure the taper of the pots does not throw the stencil out of alignment.

5 Now secure your stencil over the top of your design in the same place as before, using masking tape. This time you are going to use a coat of silver over the top of the white. The white paint acts as an undercoat and will help define the silver. Dip your stencil brush into silver paint, dab the excess onto a paper towel, and apply the paint to the stencil. Once finished, remove the stencil carefully so as not to smudge the paint and allow to dry.

6 Repeat step 5 to continue the design around the edge of the pepper pot, remembering to let your design dry in between.

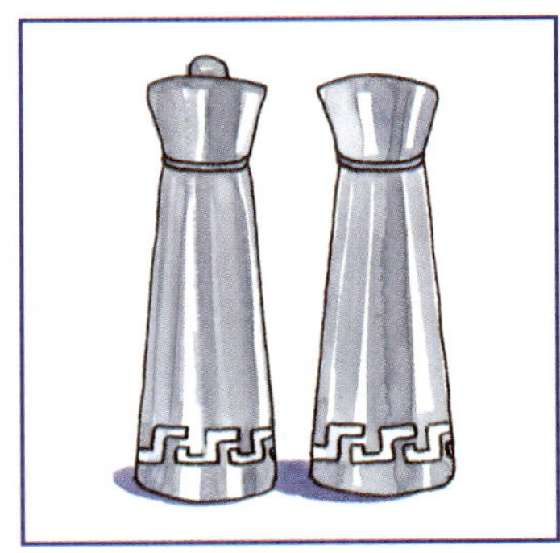

7 Copy steps 3–6 on your salt pot so that you have two identical designs.

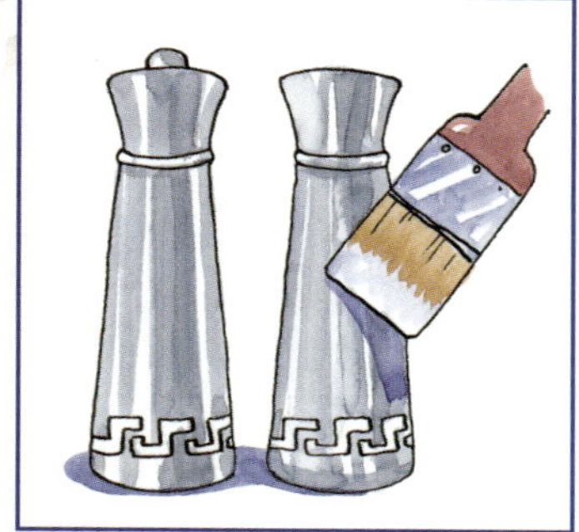

8 *Allow all the paint to dry completely, then apply a coat of gloss acrylic varnish over the entire outside of your finished pots.*

Tip: chrome effect tableware is easy to obtain, so why not continue this design on a teapot or dish? If you are going to expand the range, consider using either specialist paint for metal, or perhaps car spray paint. Remember to work in a well-ventilated area whenever you use spray paints.

TEMPLATE AND COLOR GUIDE

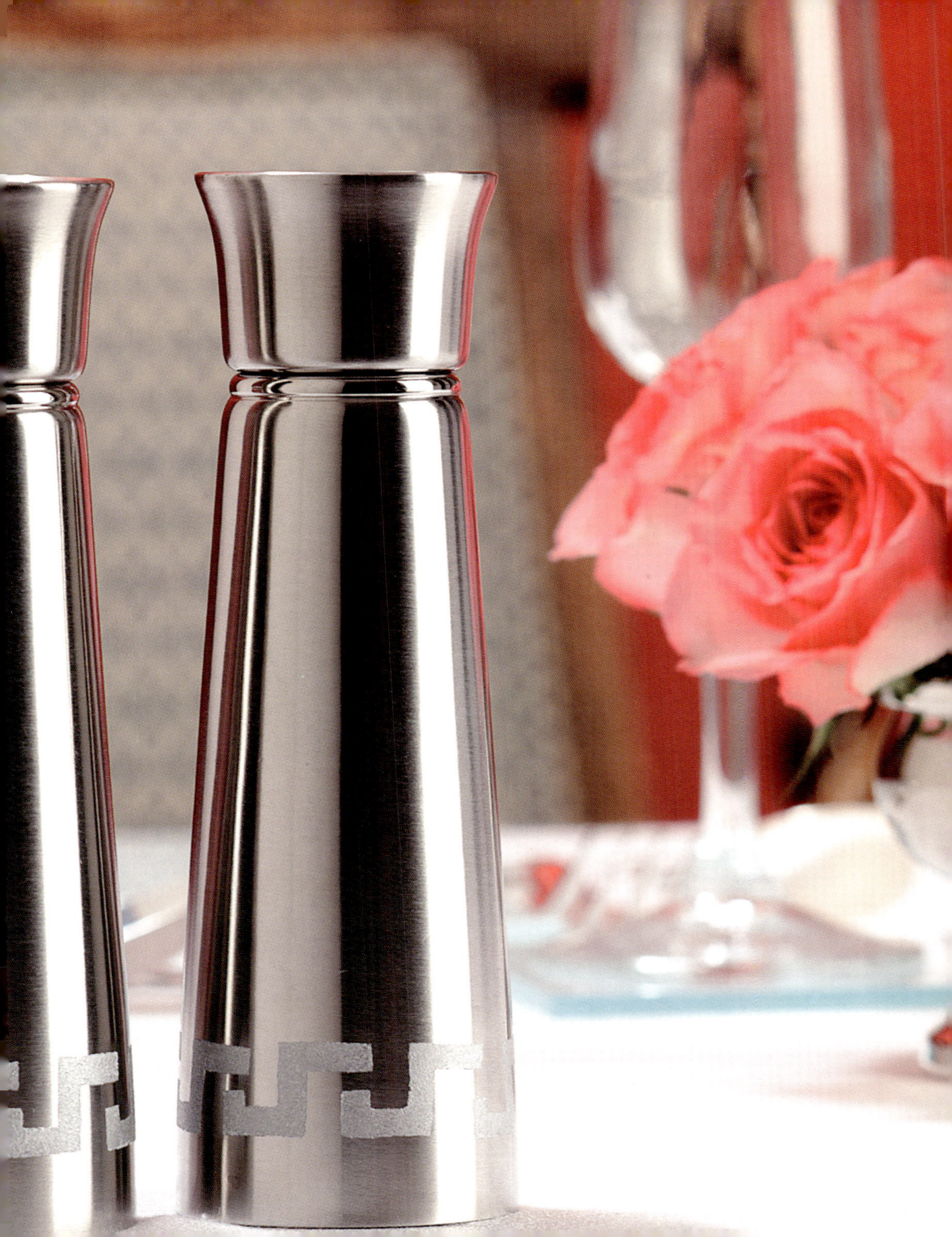

Light up your Life

Brighten up your living space by applying a simple motif to a plain lampshade. Why not make a real difference to your bedroom and continue the design of your choice on curtains or cushions? Remember to keep fabrics taut while applying the paint.

YOU WILL NEED:

- *a lampshade and lamp base*
- *gold acrylic craft paint*
- *masking tape*
- *stencil card*
- *a pencil*
- *a craft knife*
- *a stencil brush*
- *a paper towel*
- *a saucer for paint*

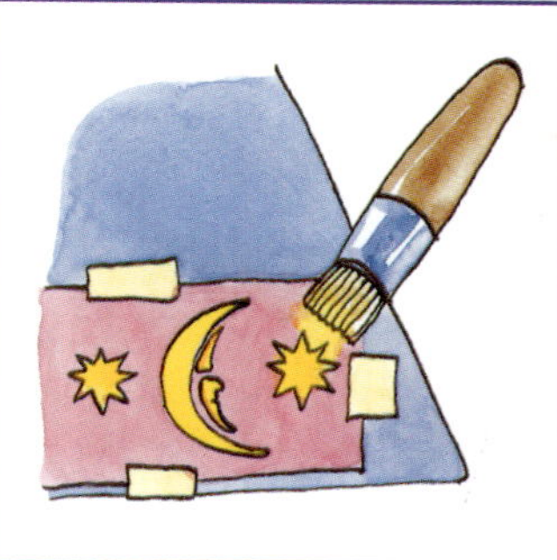

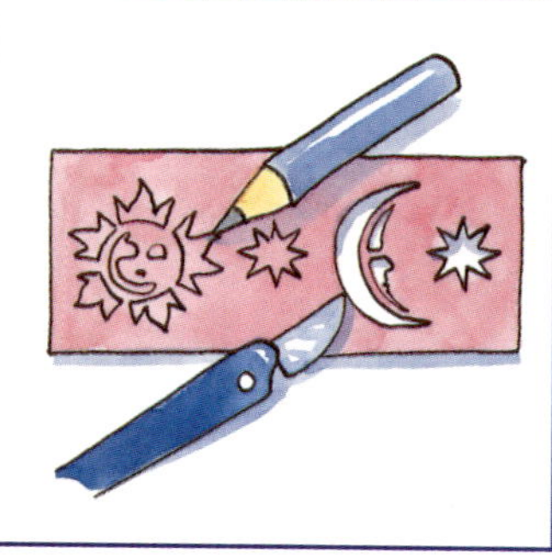

1 *To make the stencil for this design, trace over the template on page 32 onto stencil card, and carefully cut it out using a craft knife.*

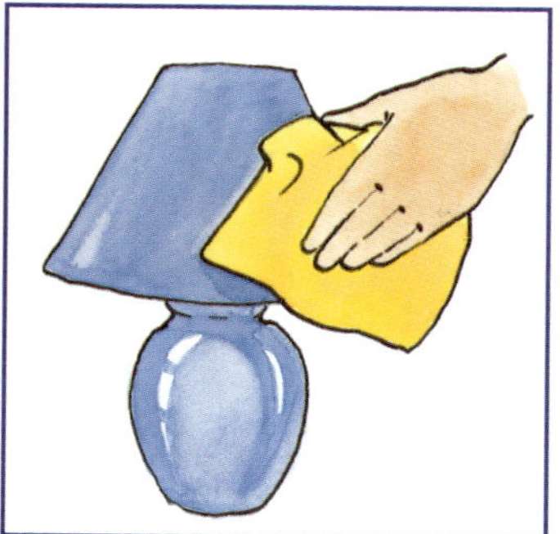

2 *Use a damp cloth to clean the lampshade and base, and allow to dry.*

3 *Place your stencil onto the lampshade about 1/2 inch from the bottom edge and secure with masking tape. Dip your stencil brush into gold paint, dab off the excess, and apply the paint to the stencil. Once finished, remove the stencil carefully and leave to dry.*

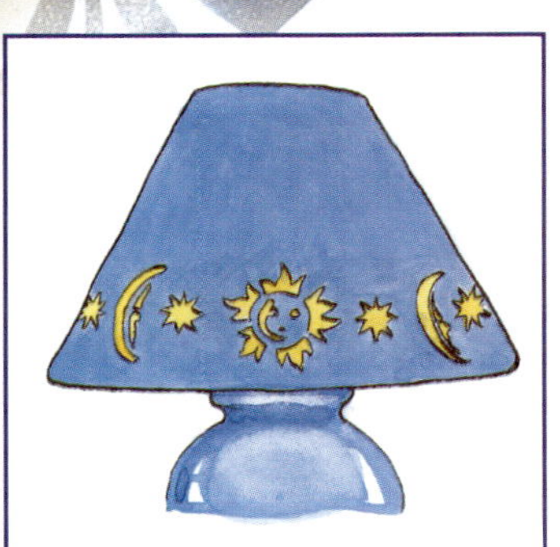

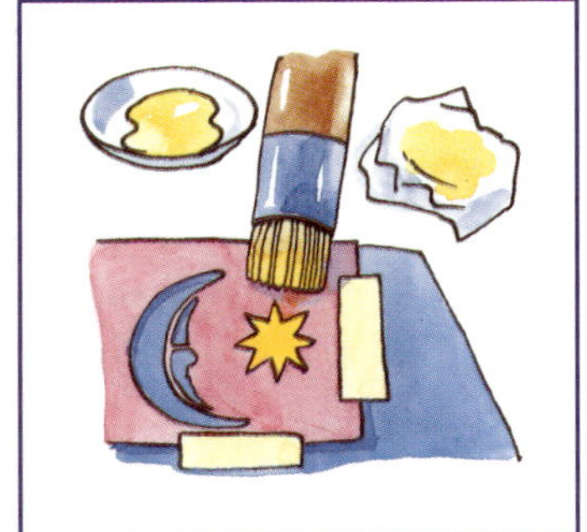

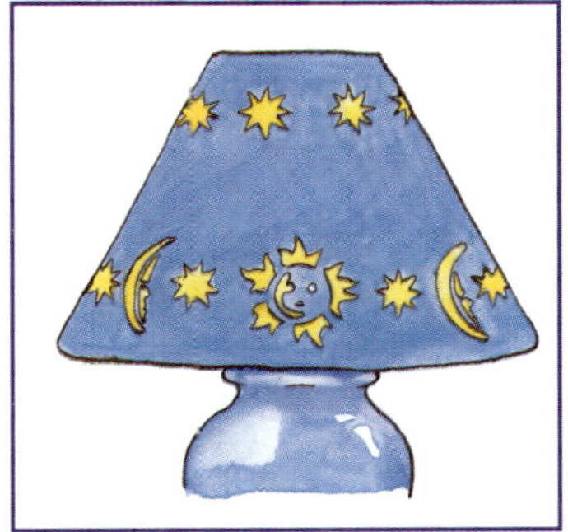

4 Repeat step 3 as many times as is needed to continue the moon and sun motif around the entire bottom edge of the lampshade, remembering to let your design dry in between.

> Tip: If you decide to repeat the design on cushions and curtains, you will need to buy fabric paint. Read the instructions before you buy, since most require either ironing or a mordant, such as vinegar or salt, to fix.

5 Now secure your stencil about 1 inch from the top edge of the lampshade using masking tape. You should only use one of the stars on the stencil for this design. Dip your stencil brush into gold paint, remove the excess onto a paper towel, and apply the paint to the stencil. Once finished, remove the stencil carefully to avoid smudging and leave to dry.

6 Repeat step 5 as many times as is needed to continue the design around the entire top edge of the lampshade, allowing the paint to dry after each stage.

> Tip: Even if your lampshade is made of fabric, it is still best to use acrylic paint as fixing any fabric paint will be difficult on a rigid object such as this.

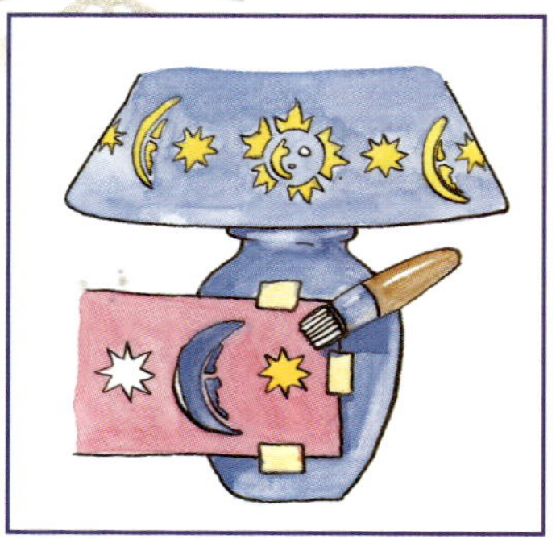

7 *For the final touch, secure the star part of the stencil in the center front of the lamp base with masking tape. Apply gold paint to your stencil brush, dab off the excess, and apply to the star.*

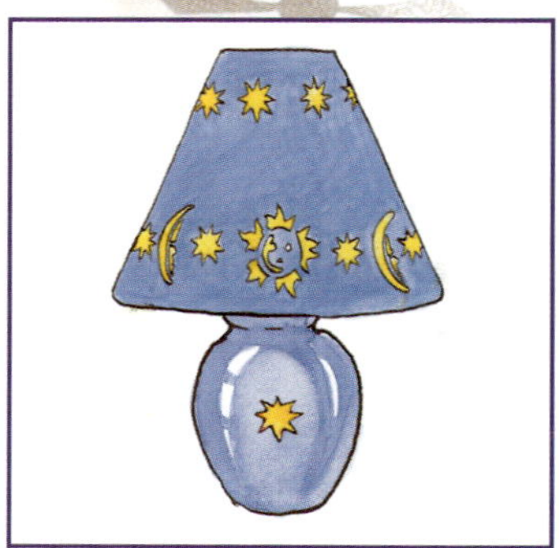

TEMPLATE AND COLOR GUIDE

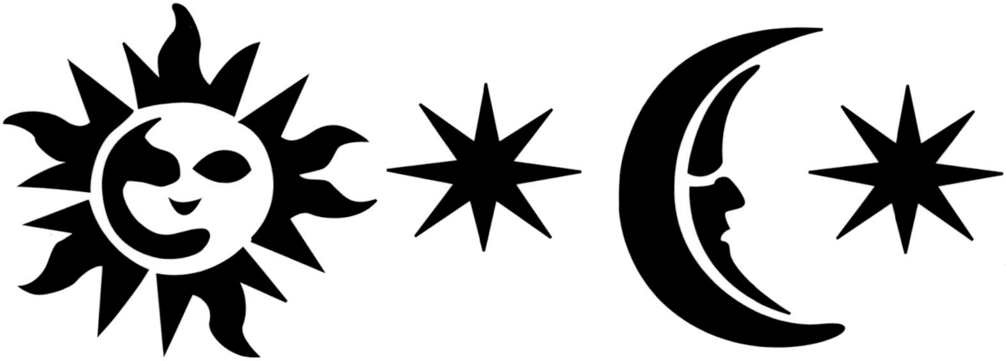

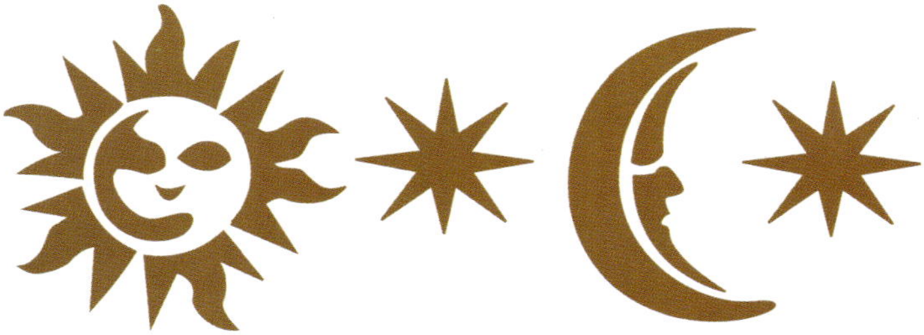

Honey to the Bee

Enhance the natural beauty of your plants with pretty pots. Consider the usage of the pot when creating the design and keep it fun.

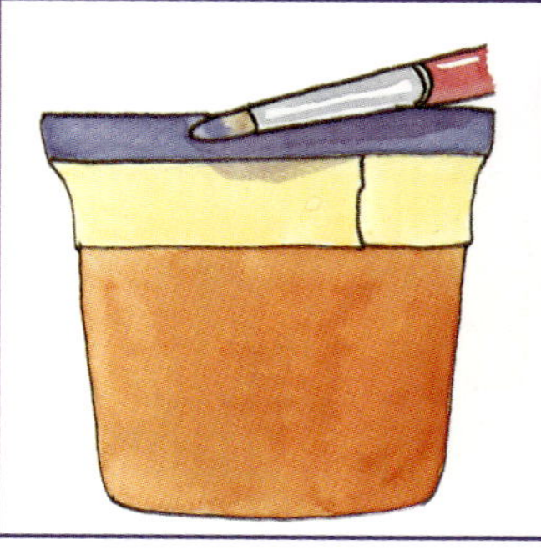

YOU WILL NEED:

- *two terra cotta plant pots*
- *red, yellow, and blue acrylic craft paint*
- *masking tape*
- *stencil card and a pencil*
- *a craft knife*
- *a stencil brush*
- *a fine paintbrush*
- *a paper towel*
- *a saucer for paint*
- *matt acrylic varnish*
- *a brush for varnishing*

For the main pot design:

3 *Leaving a gap of about 1/2 inch from the top of the pot, wrap a length of masking tape around the rim. Fill in this area with blue paint, using a fine paintbrush. Allow to dry before applying a second coat.*

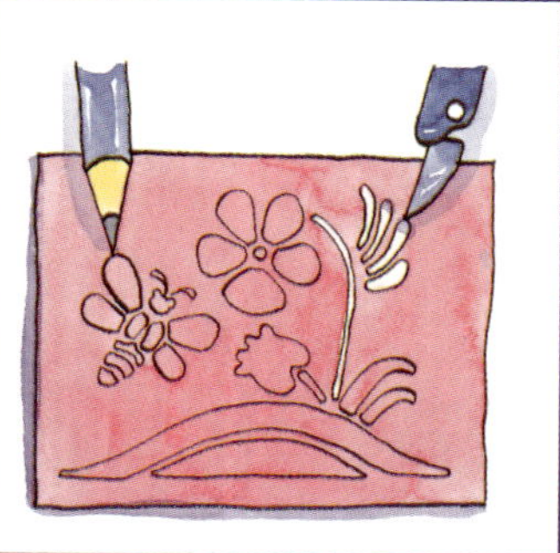

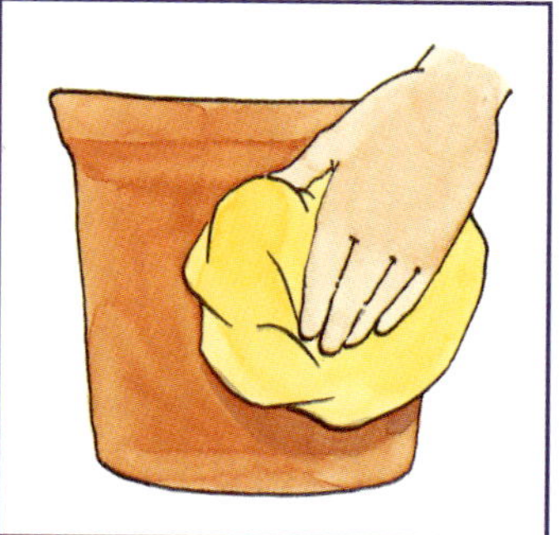

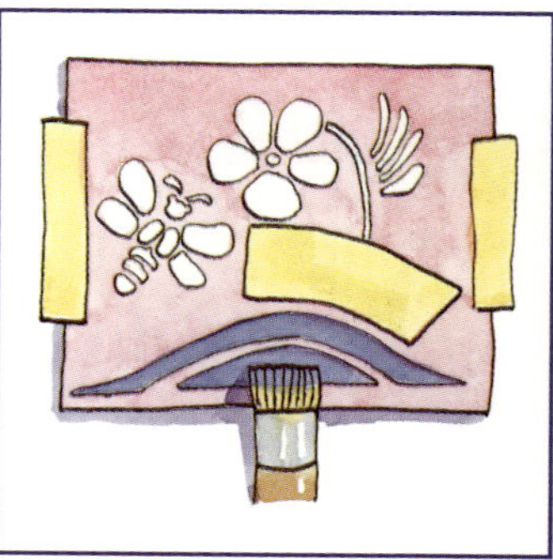

1 *To make the stencil for this design, trace over the template on page 36 onto stencil card, and carefully cut it out using a craft knife.*

2 *Wipe your plant pots free of dust and dirt using a damp cloth, and dry thoroughly.*

4 *Place the stencil onto the pot and secure with masking tape. Dip your stencil brush into blue paint, remove the excess, and apply the paint to the base of the stencil.*

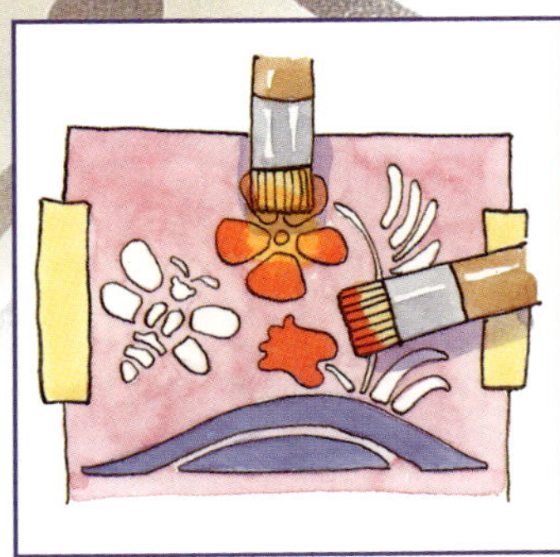

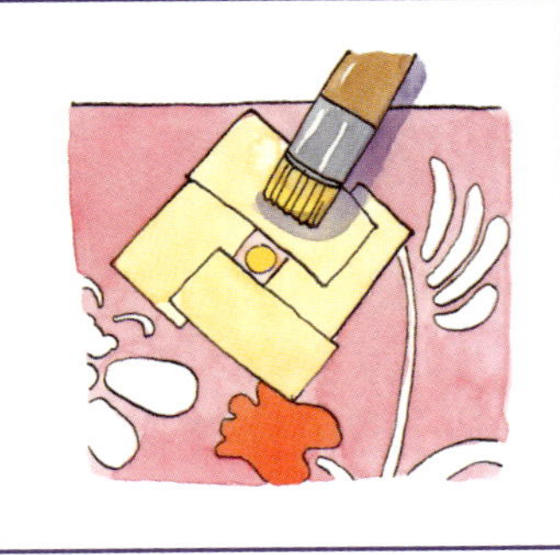

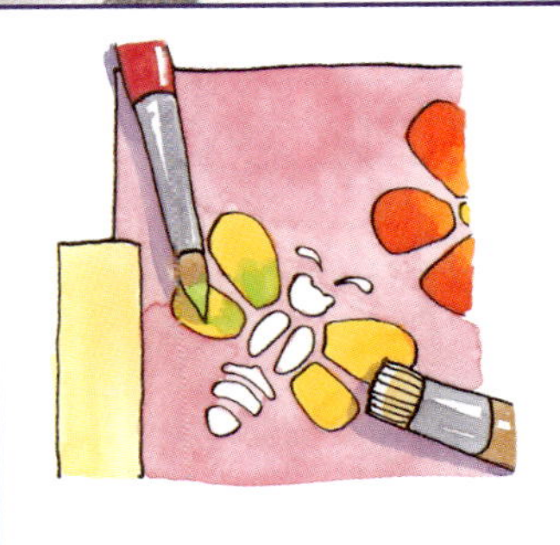

5 To paint the flowers you will need red, yellow, and a little orange mixed in a saucer. Start by painting both flowers red. Now, on the open flower, use a little of the orange paint to lighten the center of each of the petals. Leave to dry.

6 Mask off the petals of the flower with masking tape to prevent over-painting with the wrong color, and apply yellow paint to the center of the open flower.

7 To paint the bee you will need yellow, blue, and a little green mixed in a saucer. Use the yellow paint to cover the wings of the bee completely. With a little green paint, blend the center of the wings and leave to dry.

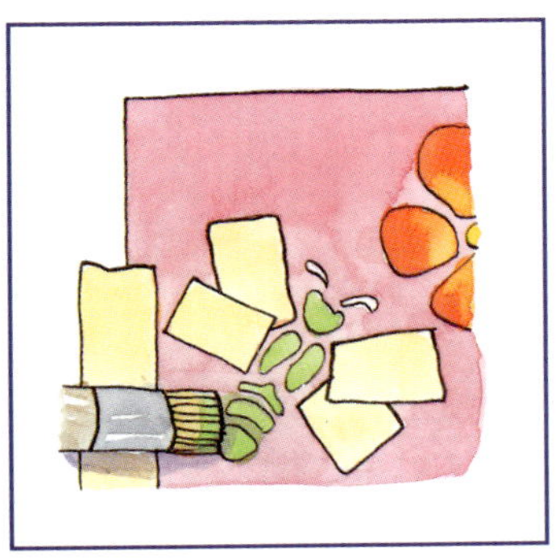

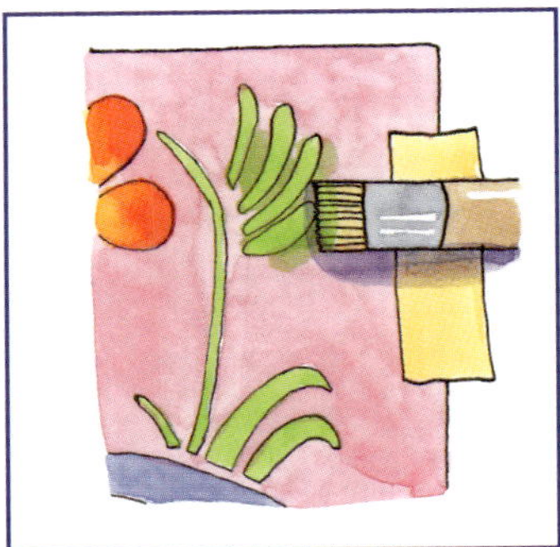

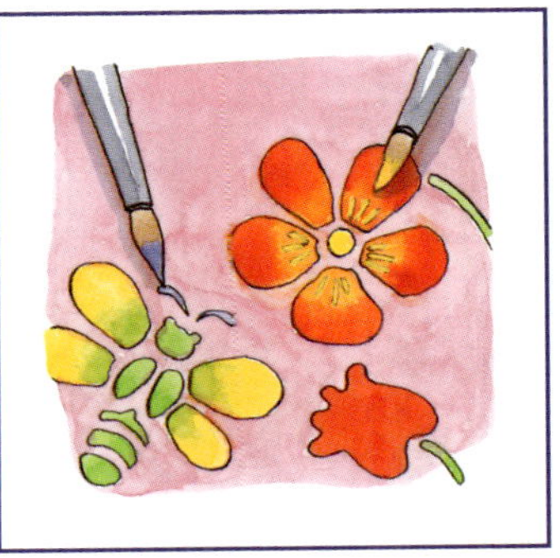

8 Mask off the wings with masking tape, then use green to paint the bee's body.

9 Still using green paint, stencil the leaves and stems of the plant. Once finished, remove the stencil carefully and allow to dry.

10 With a fine paintbrush, add yellow detail to the leaves of the open flower. Use blue paint to add antennae to the bee. Allow to dry before varnishing.

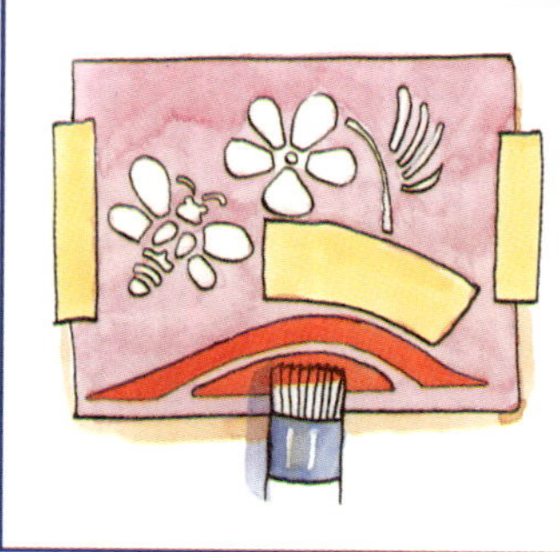

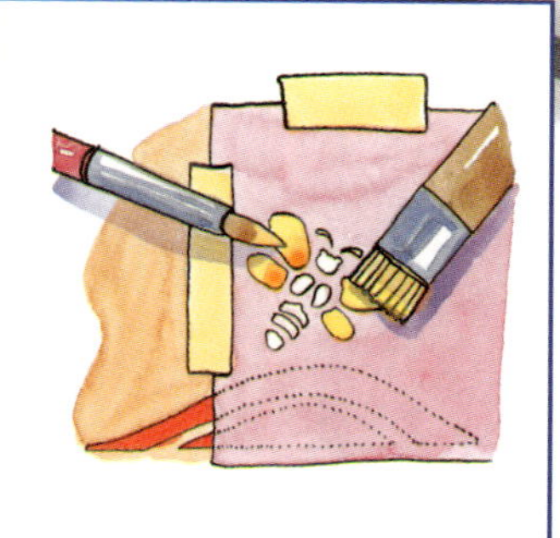

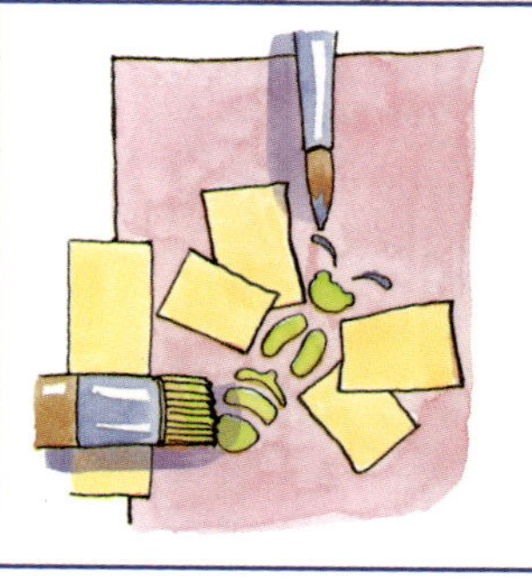

For the bee pot:

1 *Paint the rim in the same way as before, but this time use red paint. Once dry, secure the stencil onto the pot with masking tape. Dip your stencil brush into red paint and apply to the base of the stencil. Remove the stencil carefully and allow to dry.*

2 *Reposition the stencil so that the bee is over the center of the red base, and secure with masking tape. To paint the bee you will need yellow, orange, and green in a saucer. Use the yellow paint for the wings before blending a small amount of orange in the center.*

3 *When dry, mask off the wings with masking tape, then use green paint to stencil in the bee's body. Finally, add the blue antennae. Once finished, remove the stencil carefully so as not to smudge the paint, and allow to dry. Varnish once all the paint has dried.*

TEMPLATE AND COLOR GUIDE

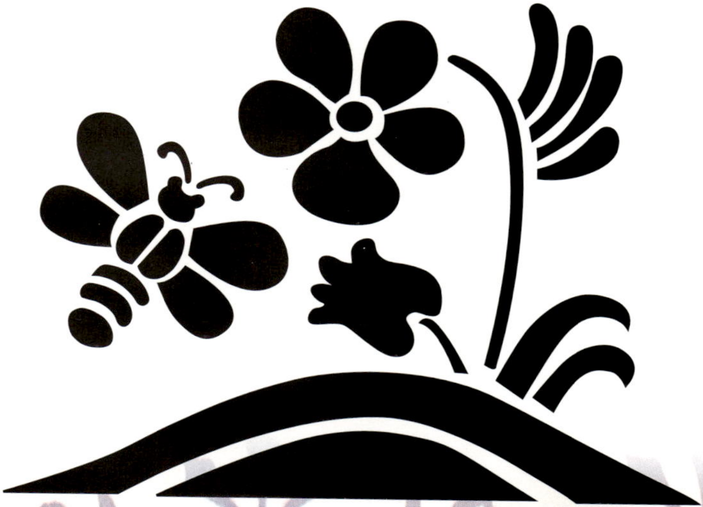

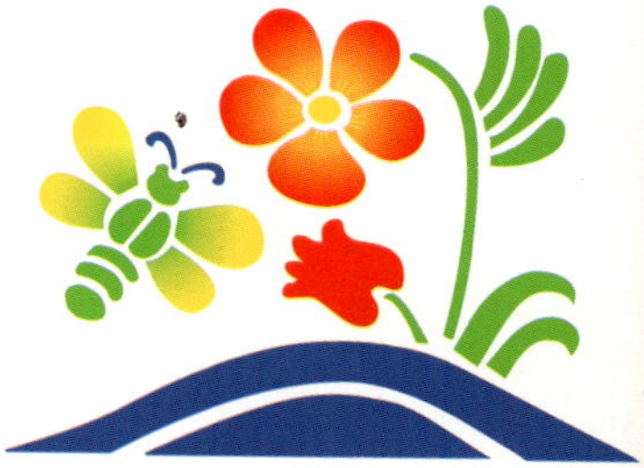

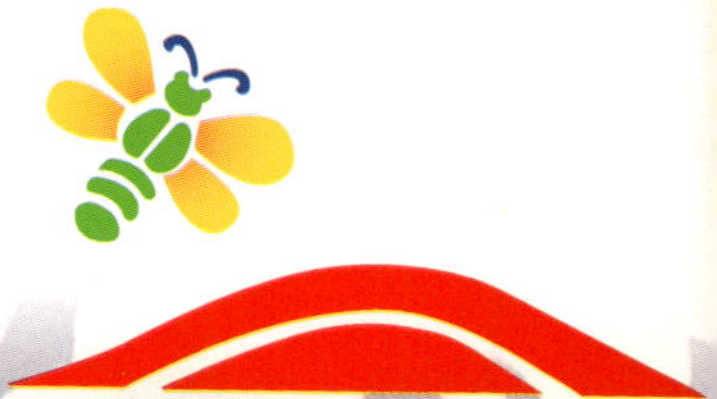

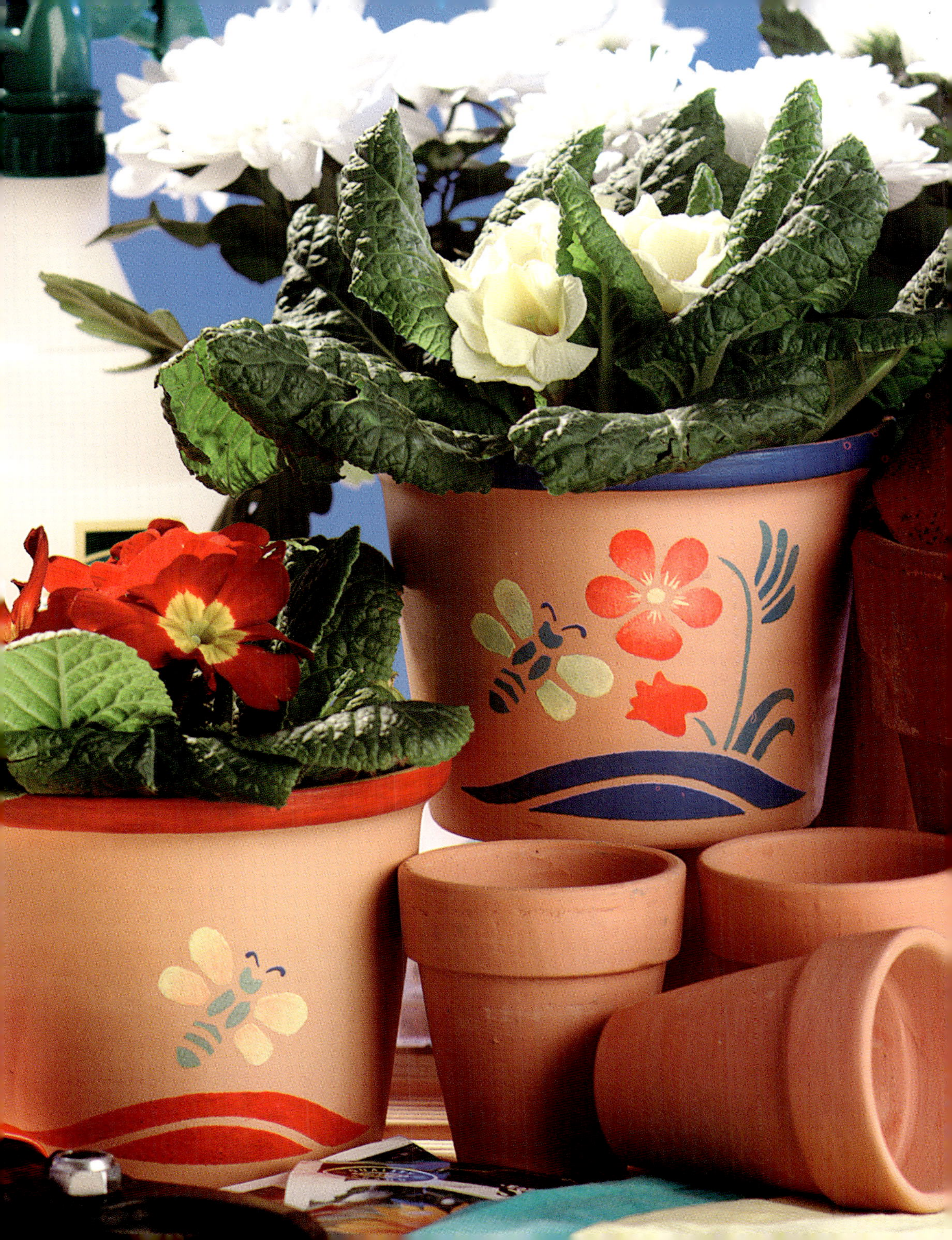

Teatime Treat

Wood is great for stenciling on, so use this tray project as a starting point. From there you can go on to decorate chairs, dressers, chests, tables, cupboards, and more.

YOU WILL NEED:

- *a large wooden tray*
- *red, yellow, blue, and black acrylic craft paint*
- *masking tape*
- *stencil card*
- *a craft knife*
- *a stencil brush*
- *a pencil*
- *a ruler*
- *a fine paintbrush*
- *a paper towel*
- *a saucer for paint*
- *matt acrylic varnish*
- *a brush for varnishing*

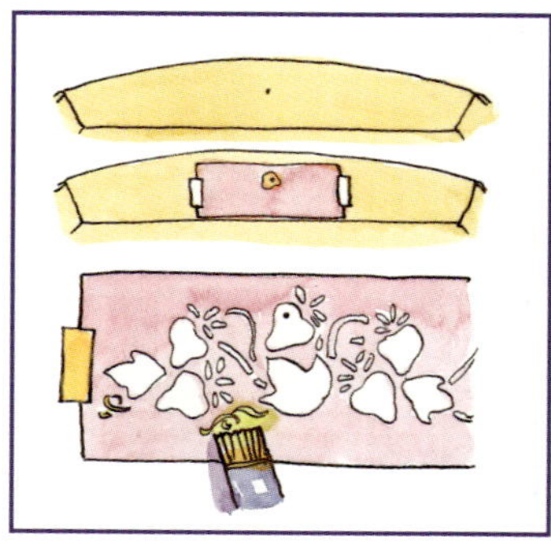

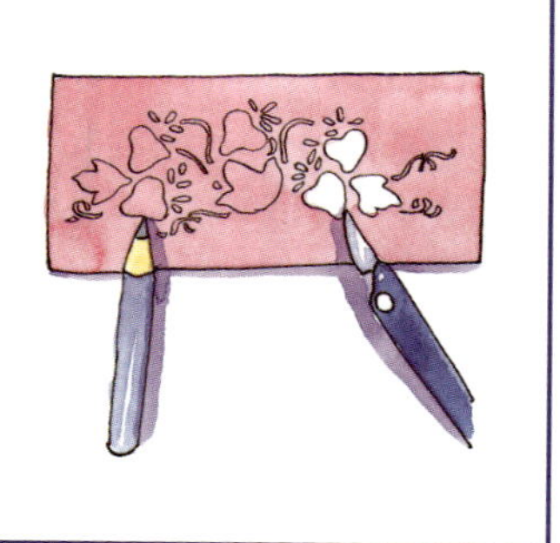

1 *To make the stencil for this design, trace over the template on page 40 onto stencil card, and carefully cut it out using a craft knife.*

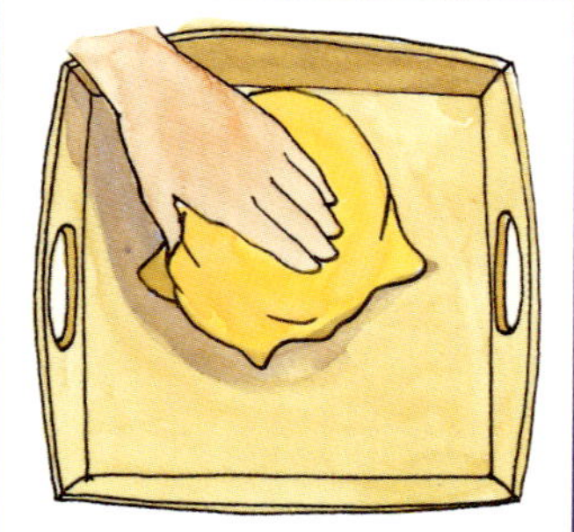

2 *Wipe your wooden tray free of dust and dirt using a damp cloth and dry thoroughly.*

For the main side design:

3 *With a ruler, measure the center point of one of the main sides and make a small dot with a pencil. Place the stencil onto the tray so that it is central, and secure with masking tape. In a saucer, use the blue and yellow paint to mix a light green and a slightly darker green. Use the light green first to paint in the wispy curls on the stencil.*

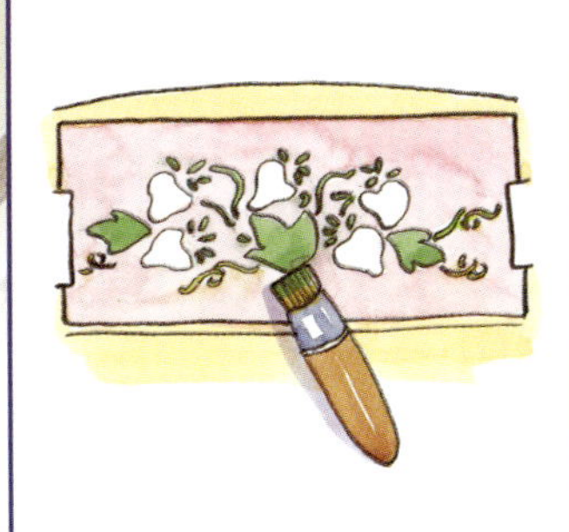

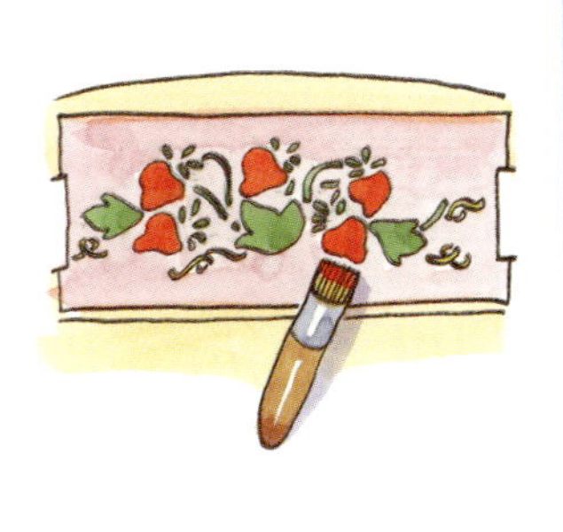

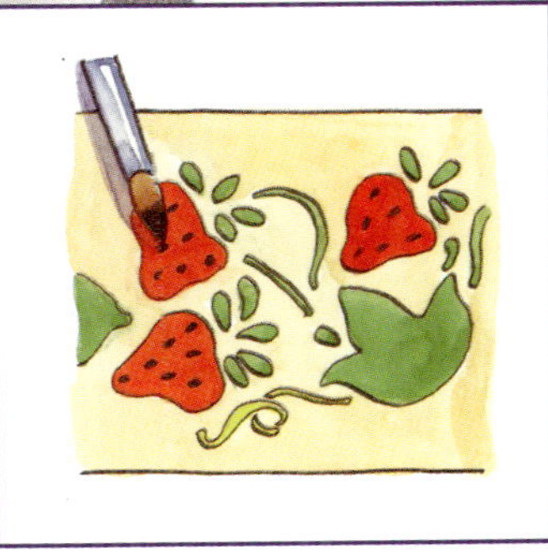

4 Apply some of the darker green to your stencil brush. Cover all the strawberry leaves and fruit heads, leaving the five strawberries untouched.

5 Paint the strawberries using the red paint. When finished, carefully remove the stencil so as not to smudge the paint, and allow to dry completely.

6 With a fine paintbrush and black paint, add detail to the strawberries with tiny dots.

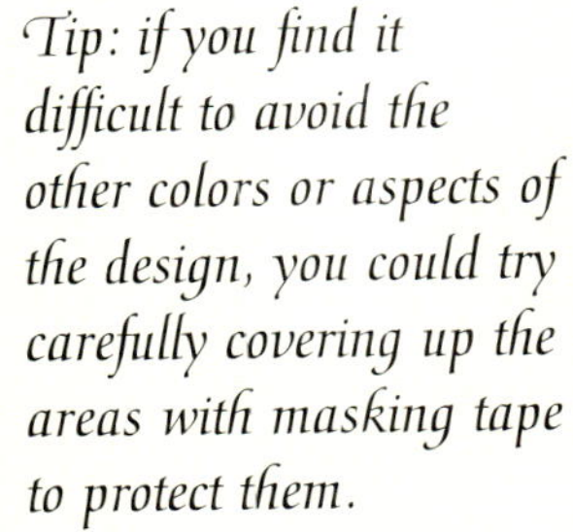

Tip: if you find it difficult to avoid the other colors or aspects of the design, you could try carefully covering up the areas with masking tape to protect them.

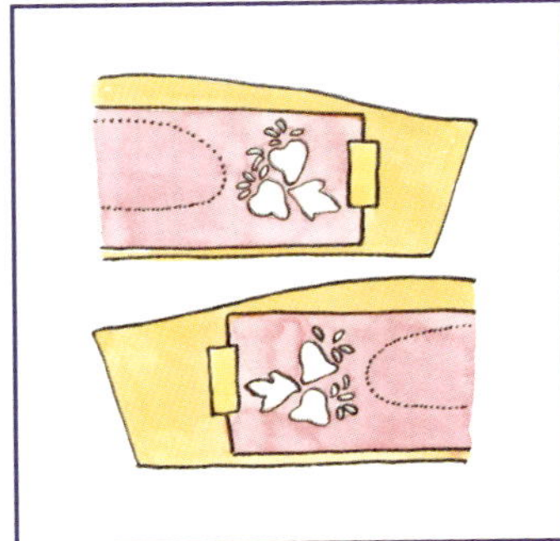

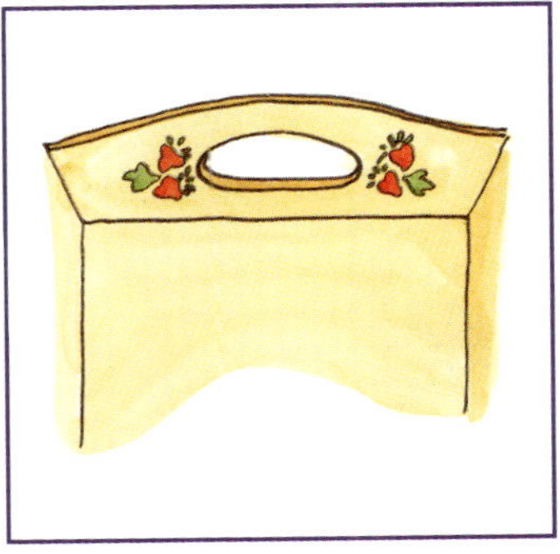

TEMPLATE FOR TRAY HANDLE

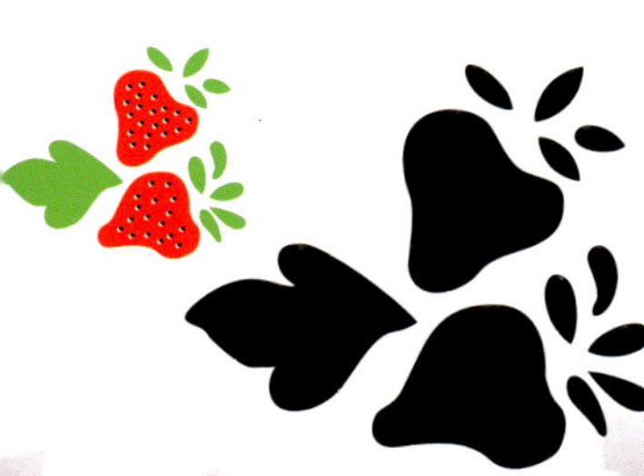

7 For the handle design, copy the template shown on the left. Simply flipping the stencil card will reverse the design for the other side of the handle.

8 With the stencil in place, follow steps 3–6 to complete the motif on each handle.

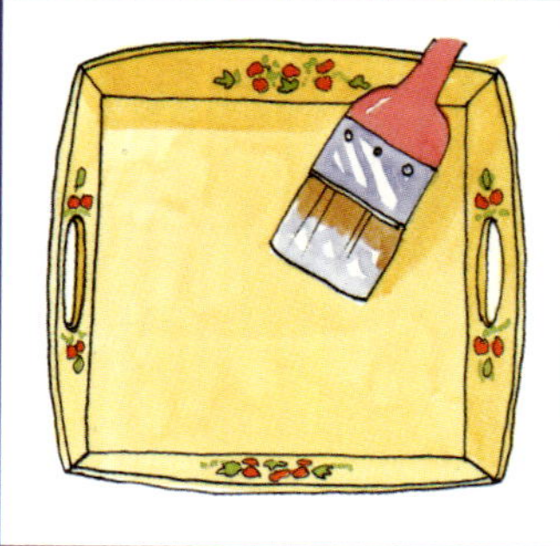

Tip: Always wash and dry your stencil brush thoroughly before using a different color.

9 Allow all paint to dry completely, then apply a coat of matt acrylic varnish over all the sides of your finished tray. This will protect your design and give it a more hard-wearing and permanent finish.

Future project ideas: Stylized slices of other fruits such as oranges, limes, and watermelon would look equally good on kitchen items. If your favorite design is these strawberries, then consider enlarging the design with a copier and applying to chairs or as a border to a kitchen table.

TEMPLATE AND COLOR GUIDE

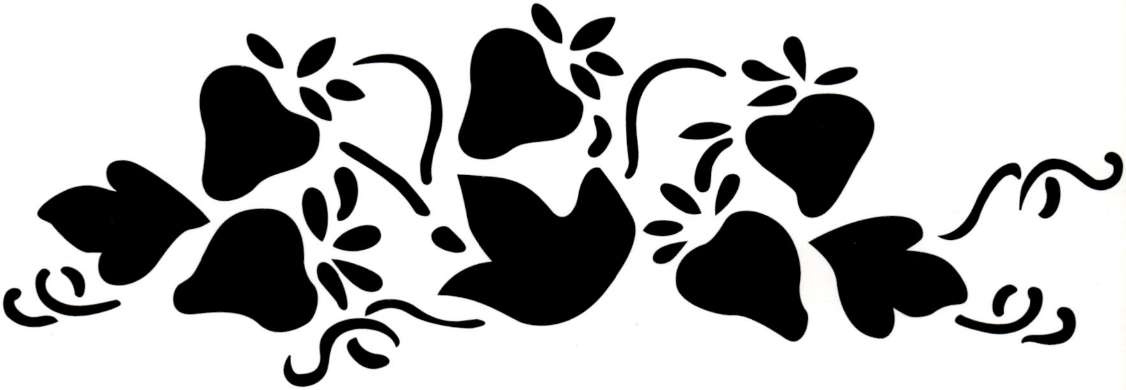

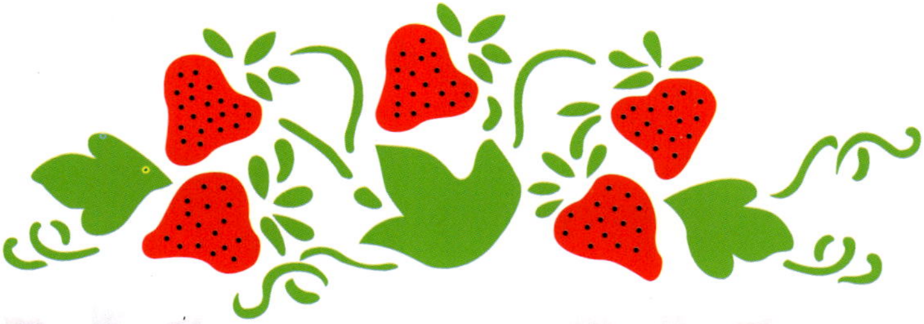

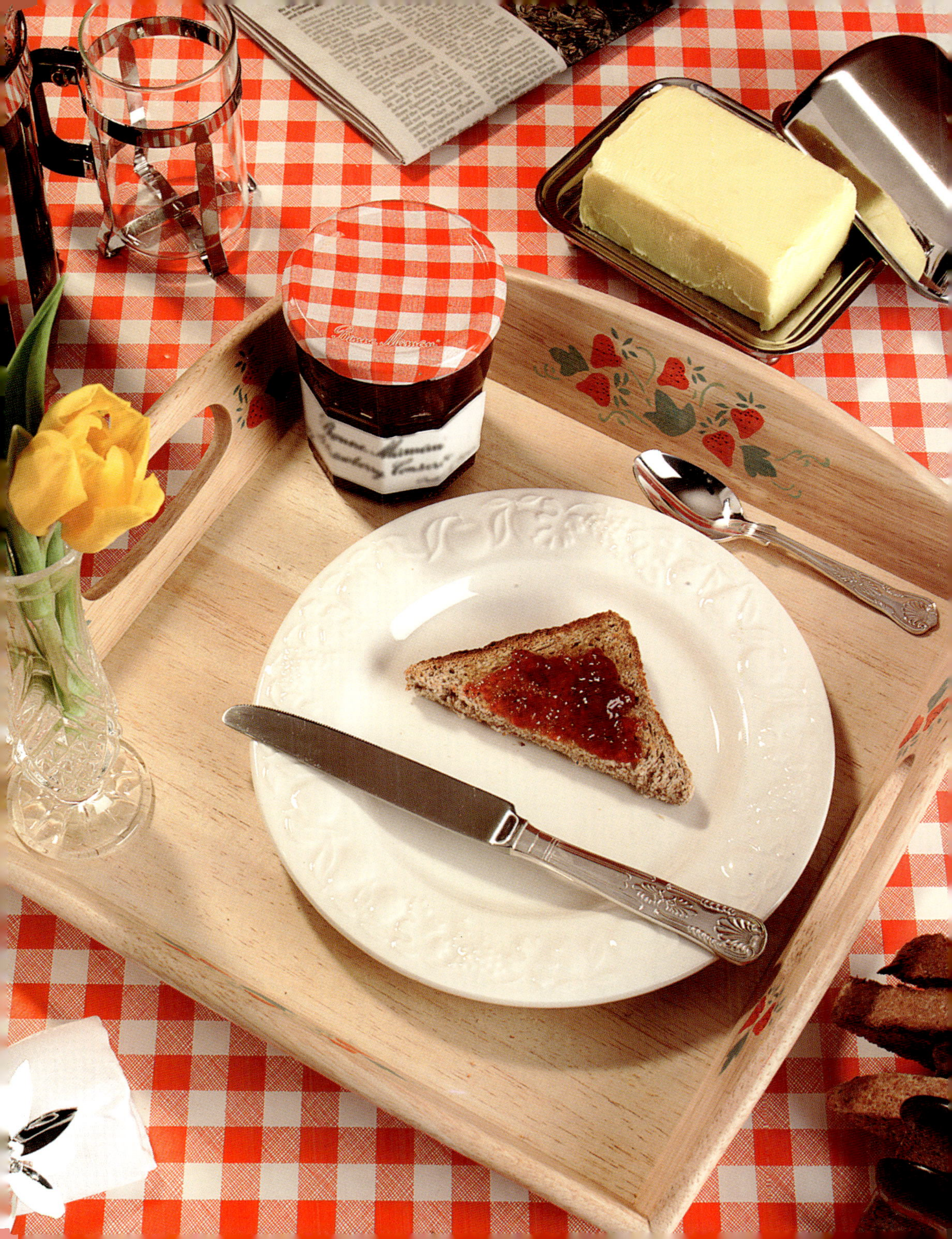

Styles for Tiles

Whether decorating tiles in the kitchen or bathroom, stencils are a great way of stamping your own style on what can often be an overlooked wall covering.

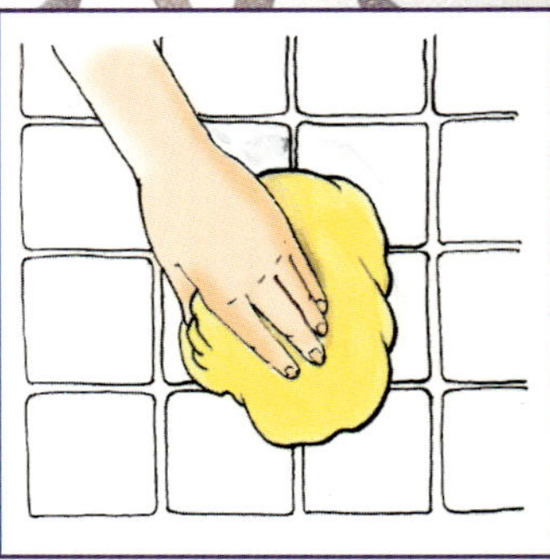

3 *Wipe your tiles free of dust and dirt using a damp cloth and dry thoroughly.*

YOU WILL NEED:

- *4 inch square tiles*
- *red, white, yellow, blue, and silver acrylic paint*
- *masking tape*
- *stencil card*
- *a craft knife*
- *a pencil*
- *a stencil brush*
- *a paper towel*
- *a saucer for paint*
- *gloss acrylic varnish*
- *a brush for varnishing*

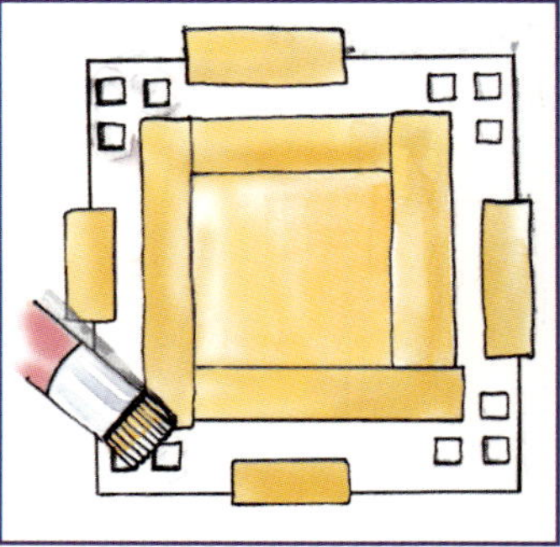

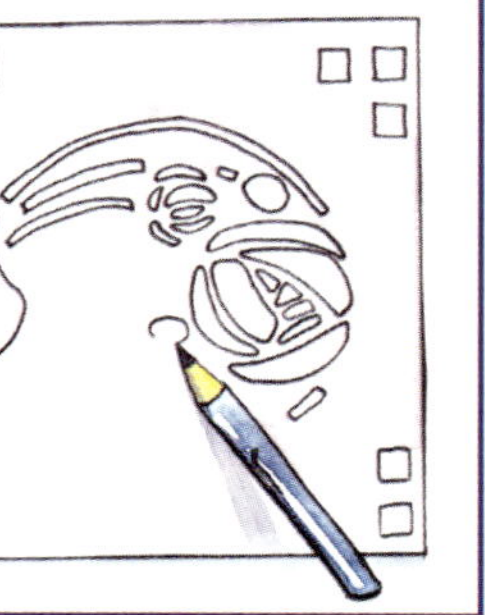

1 *To make the stencil for this design, trace over the template on page 44 onto stencil card.*

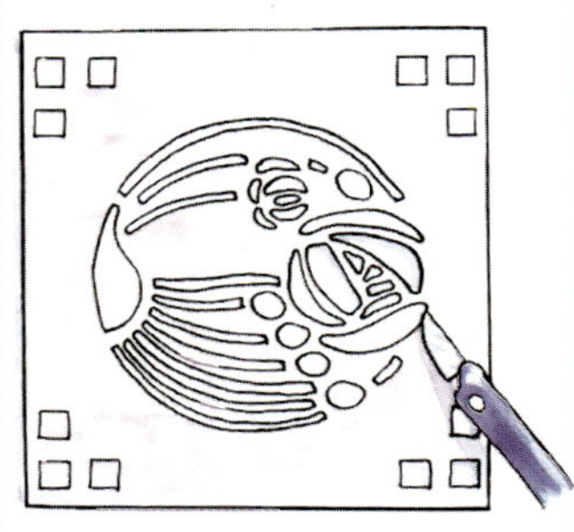

2 *Carefully cut out your design using a craft knife.*

For the squares:

4 *Using masking tape, mask off the center flower design from your stencil, leaving only the three squares in each corner. Fix the stencil on the first tile with masking tape.*

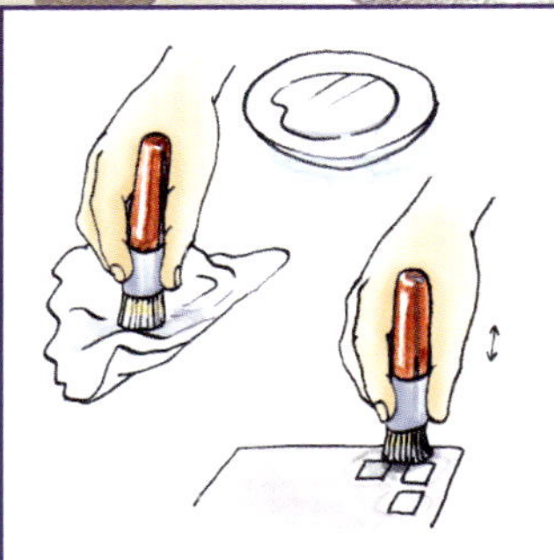

5 Dip your stencil brush into the silver paint, dab the excess onto a paper towel, and apply the paint to the stencil. Remove the stencil when the paint has completely dried. Repeat the pattern over the other tiles.

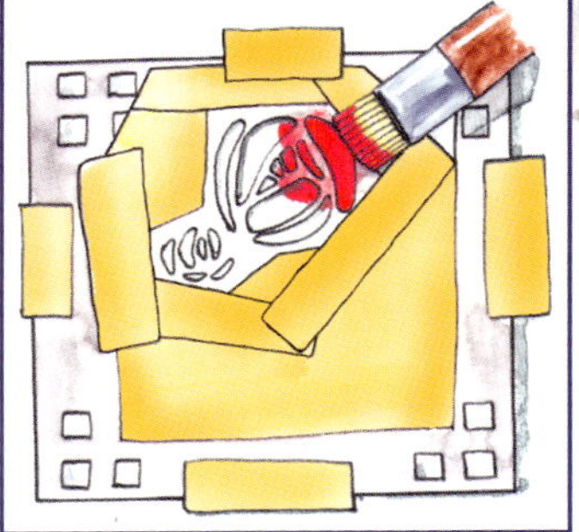

For the flower design:

6 Mask off all of the design, except for the two rose heads, and secure the stencil. Mix the red and white paint together and apply the pink paint to all the rose petals.

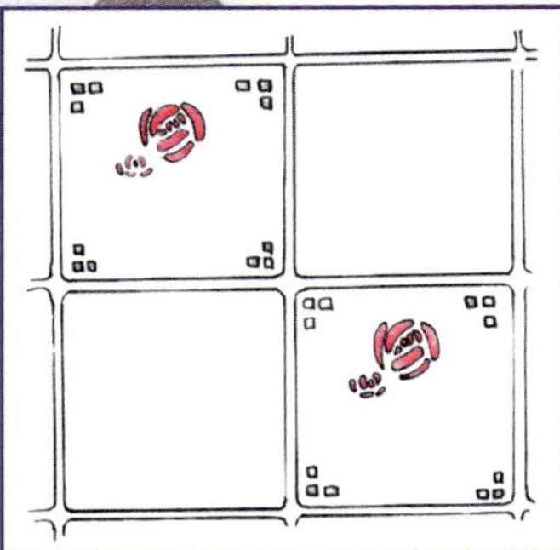

7 Repeat this for each of the flower tiles in your pattern.

Tips:

- You can vary the shades of pink by adding more white paint to create a less uniform look.
- Leave the corner squares unmasked and you can use them to center your design each time you apply a different color.

Warning: Be careful not to press too hard with the masking tape. You don't want it to stick to the paint already on your tile. Alternatively, you can buy low-tack masking tape from good DIY stores.

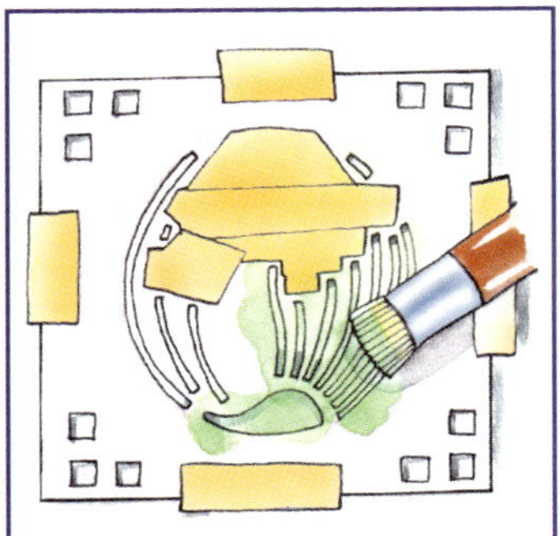

8 Now, mask off everything leaving the stems and stem base. Secure the stencil onto the tile. Dip your stencil brush into a little mixed green paint and apply it to the stencil. Allow to dry.

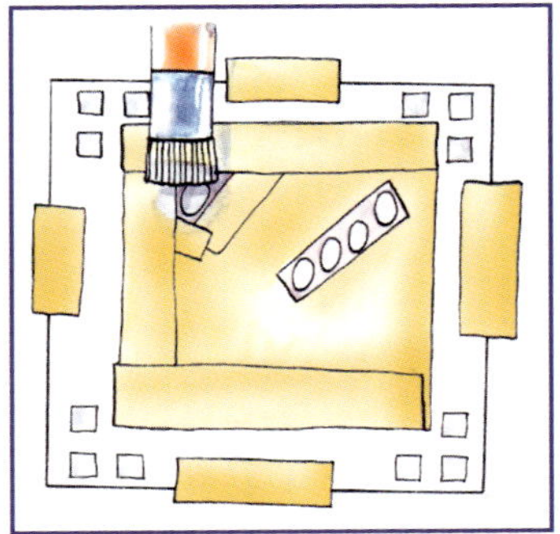

9 Finally, use your masking tape to mask off all of the design except for the five oval shapes. Use the stencil brush and silver paint to fill in the remaining oval areas.

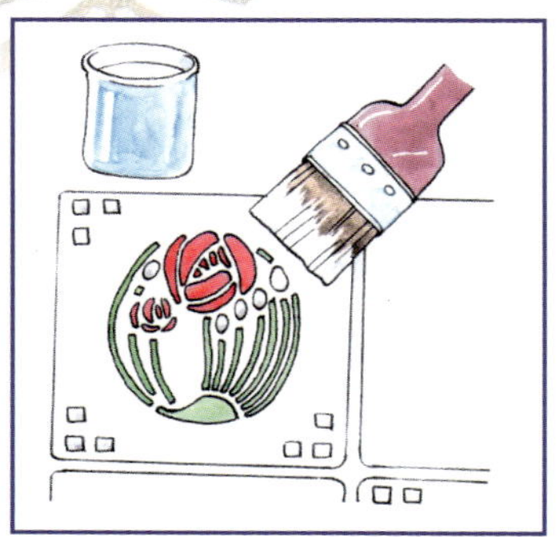

10 *Allow all paint to dry completely, then apply a coat, or two, of gloss acrylic varnish over your finished tiles. This will give your design a more hard-wearing and permanent finish and will stop your design from being scratched off.*

Tip: If you are finding it difficult to stencil straight onto the tile, apply a coat of gloss acrylic varnish first. This will provide a base for your paint to stick to. Alternatively, you could buy special tile paint. It's more expensive, but will leave you with a better finish.

TEMPLATE AND COLOR GUIDE

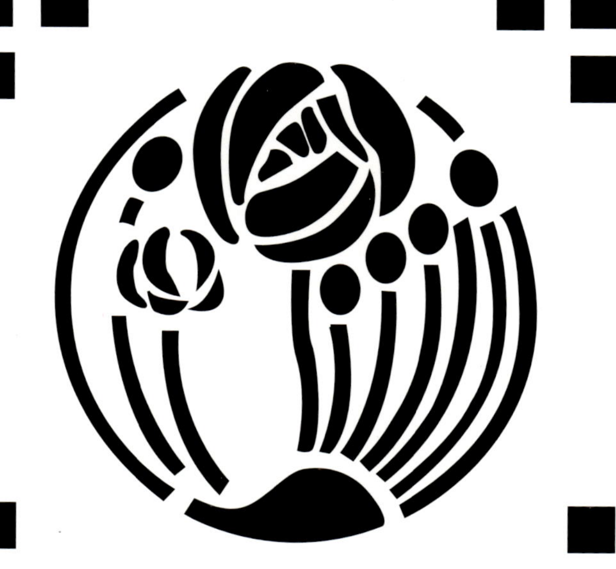

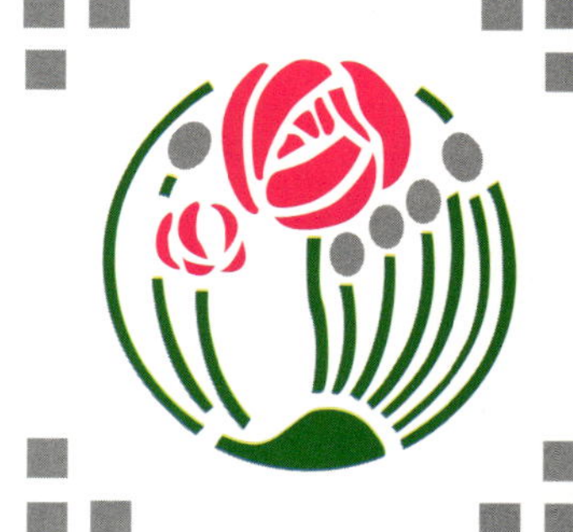

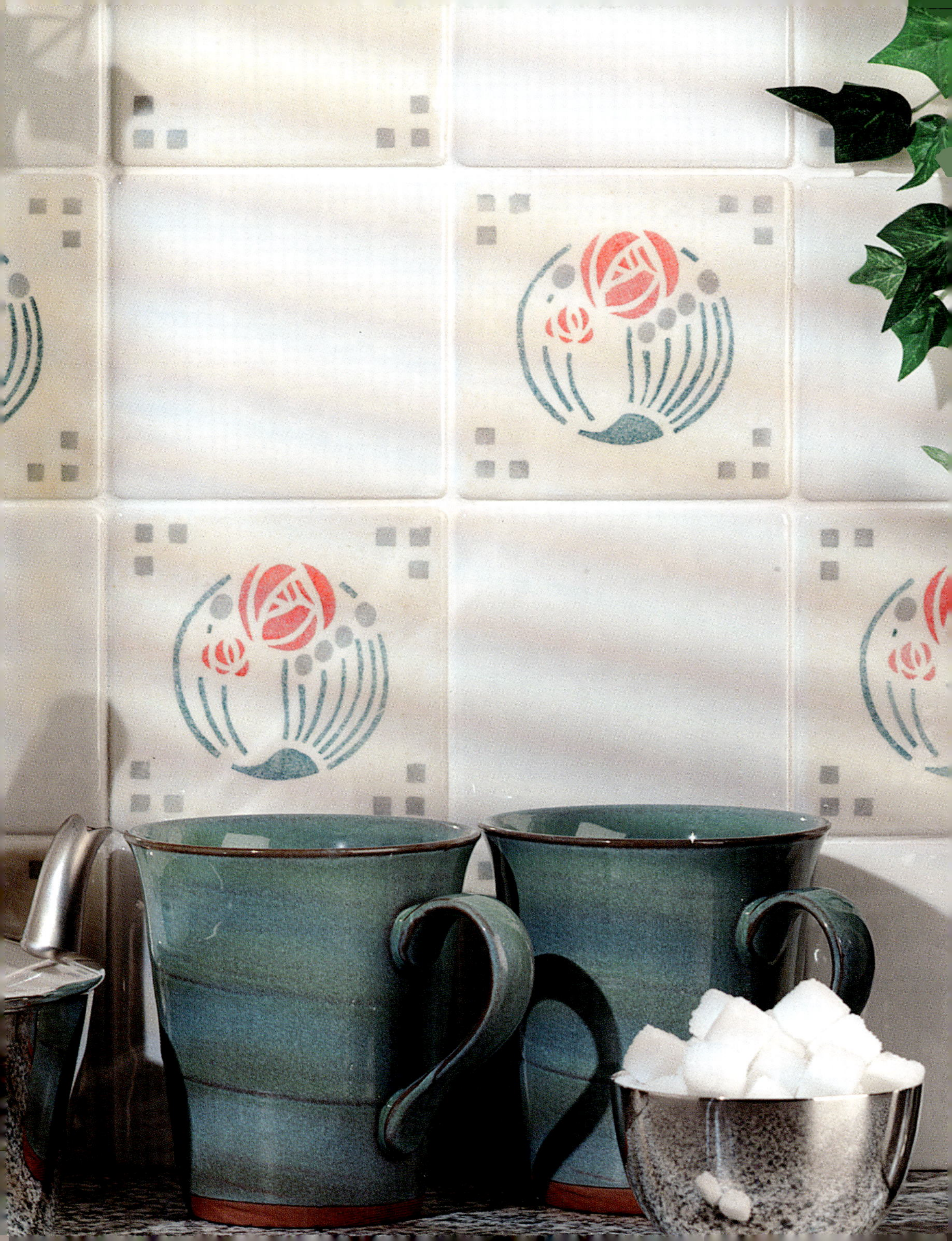

A Room with a View

Using a stencil design on walls and flooring is the perfect way to tie themes together. Take inspiration from a favorite ornament or look in interior design magazines for the latest trends.

YOU WILL NEED:

- *matt emulsion paint in the colors of your choice—the example shown in this book uses soft linen and almond cream*
- *wall sealant, if working on fresh plaster walls*
- *a paint roller and tray*
- *stencil card and a pencil*
- *primer, if working on new wood, or suitable paints for work surface*
- *acrylic paints, or similar to apply design*
- *masking tape*
- *a craft knife and pencil*
- *a stencil brush*
- *a paper towel*
- *a saucer for paint*
- *polyurethane varnish*
- *a brush for varnishing*

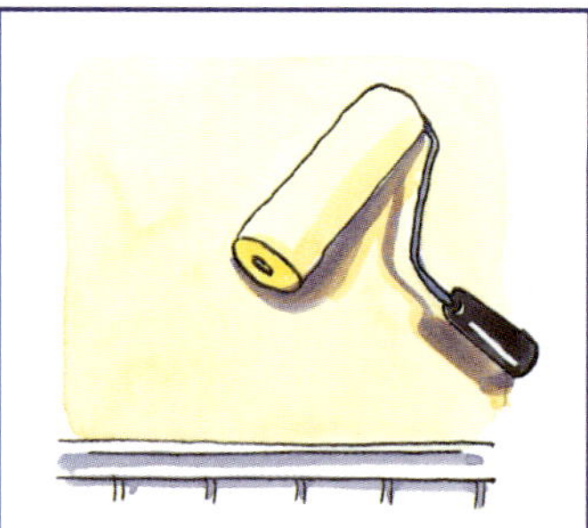

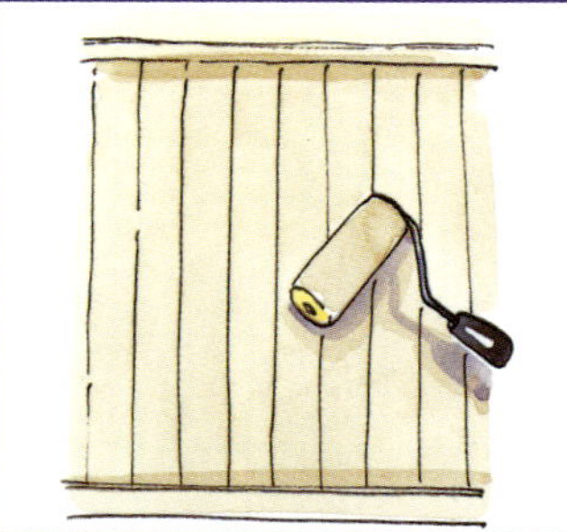

Tip: before applying emulsion to fresh plaster work be sure to seal with wall sealant or watered-down glue.

1 *Before starting, ensure the wall surfaces are smooth and clean. Prepare the wall using a matt emulsion. Fresh plaster will also need a coat of sealant.*

2 *Paint the lower half of the wall in a slightly darker tone, such as almond cream. Any new woodwork should be prepared with a primer first, however there are paints available, for certain surfaces, which do not require this extra work. Leave all paint to dry then mark the wall up (see page 16) to aid stencil positioning in step 5.*

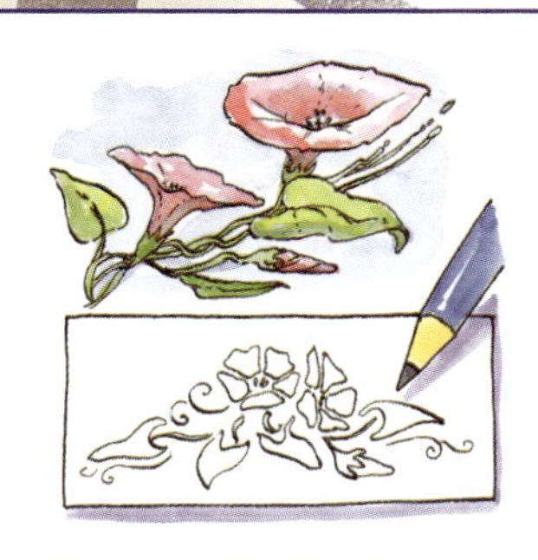

3 The next stage is to design your stencil. The design used here creates a great country cottage look, using a piece of common bindweed. Use the templates provided on page 48 if you want to recreate this project in your own home.

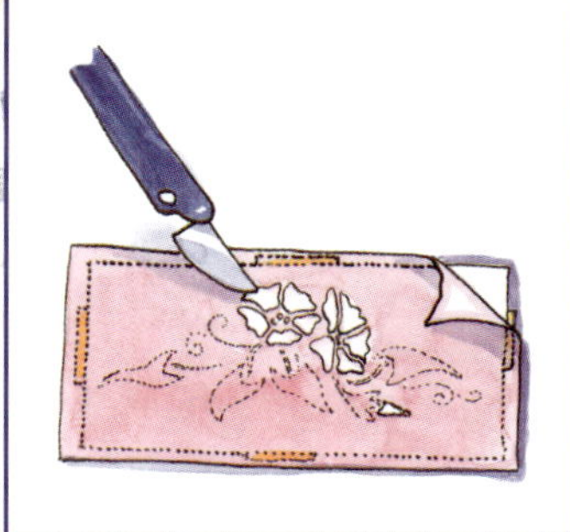

4 Transfer your design to the stencil card. With this project it is best to cut out the areas where pink, the palest color, will appear first, and stencil the design in stages, rather than cut the whole picture out first.

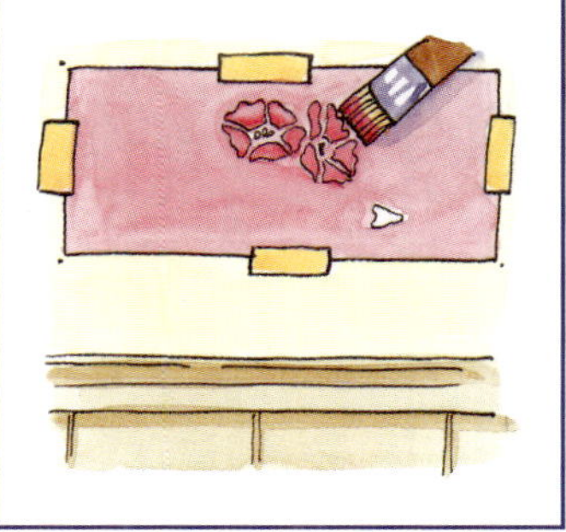

5 Use the pencil guidelines made in step 2 and secure your stencil in place. Mix up one color at a time and apply to the wall. Develop tone by applying pressure with the brush or by painting with a slightly darker tone. Always start with the palest color.

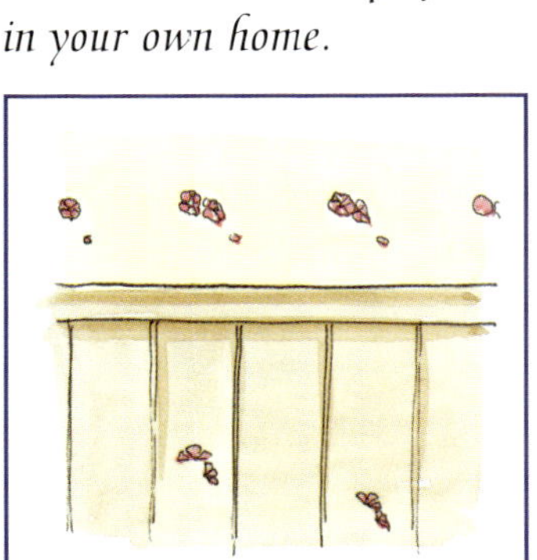

6 Repeat step 5 as many times as required. Change your stencil for the tongue and groove section of the wall, but continue working with the pale pink paint.

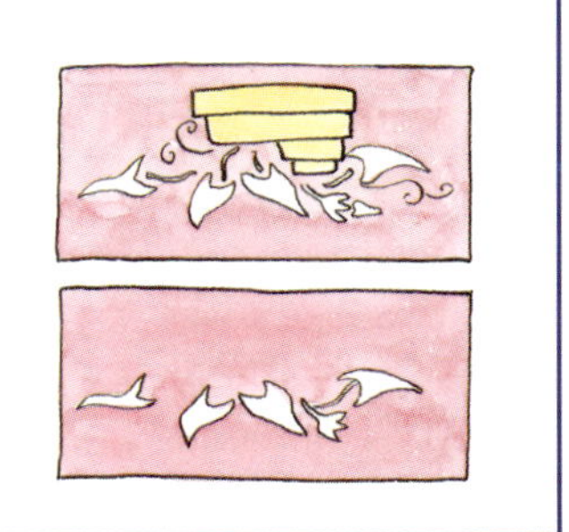

7 For subsequent colors, either cut out the corresponding sections from the stencil and mask old areas, or use a new piece of card. Secure and paint as before.

Tip: Always stencil on the walls and panels before the floor. Start from the top of the wall and work down to avoid smudging your work. Also, you don't want to be awkwardly stretching over your floor design, or risk spilling paint on finished work.

Tip: As a large room can be quite demanding, try to stick to applying one color at a time. Since the work is likely to last beyond one session, break the room into smaller sections, aiming to complete each one in turn.

8 Once the wall surfaces are finished, clean the floor surfaces and follow the same process to complete the floor design. Once the floor, walls, and panels are dry, you will need to use polyurethane varnish to protect them from wear and tear. It comes in a variety of finishes—gloss, matt, or satin—and it is extremely hard-wearing.

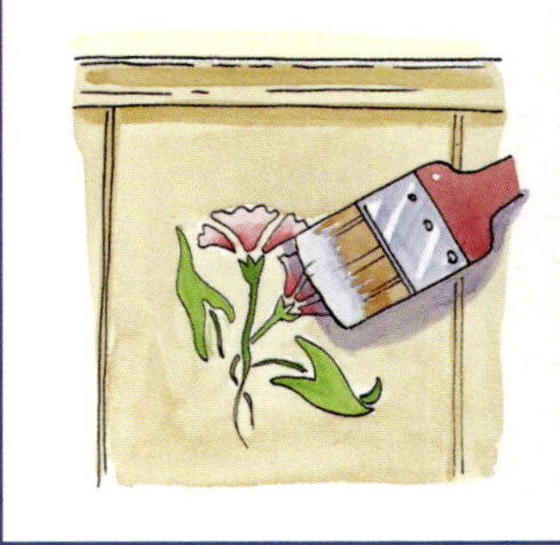

TEMPLATE AND COLOR GUIDE

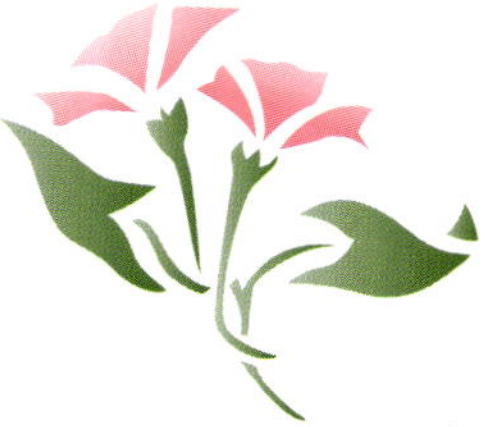

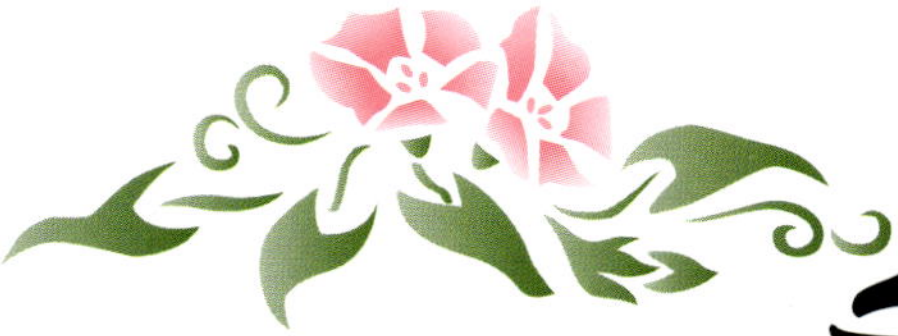

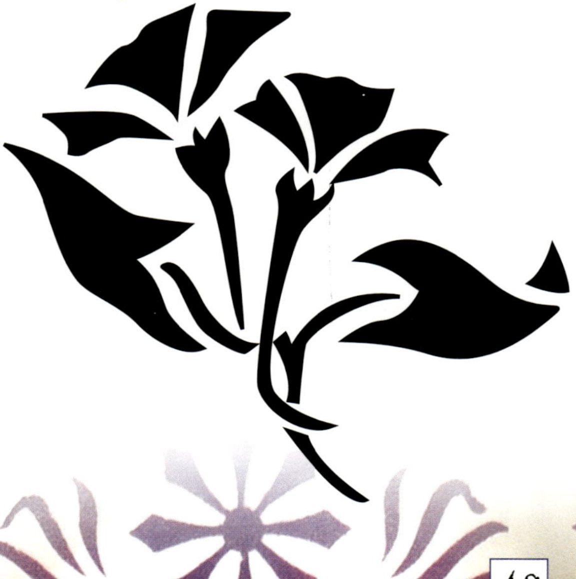

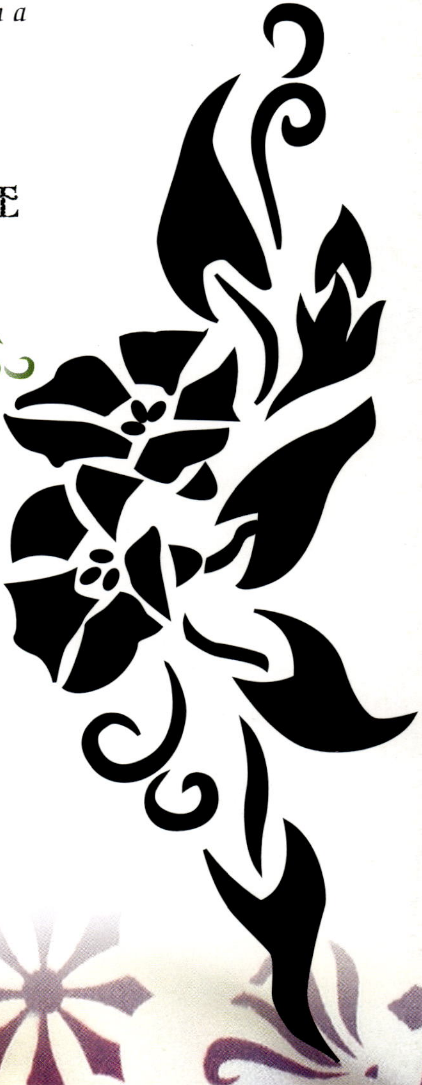

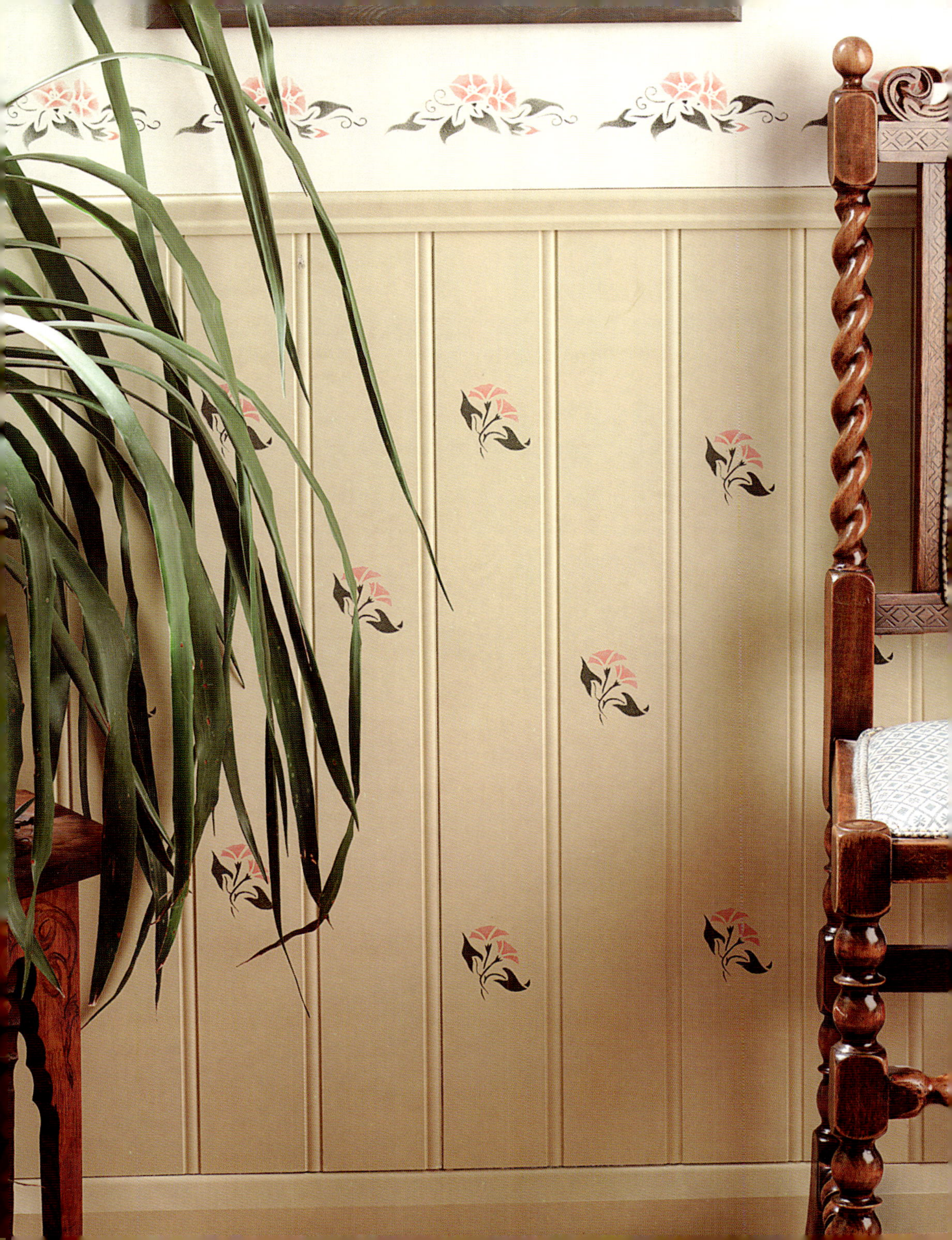

Box of Tricks

You don't need to stick to using acrylic paint in all your projects—you can get a great finish using spray paints.

YOU WILL NEED:

- *a wooden box*
- *stencil card or acetate*
- *a craft knife*
- *turpentine*
- *four cans of spray paint: gold, copper, white, and brown*
- *a cloth*
- *spray glue*
- *acrylic varnish*
- *a brush for varnishing*

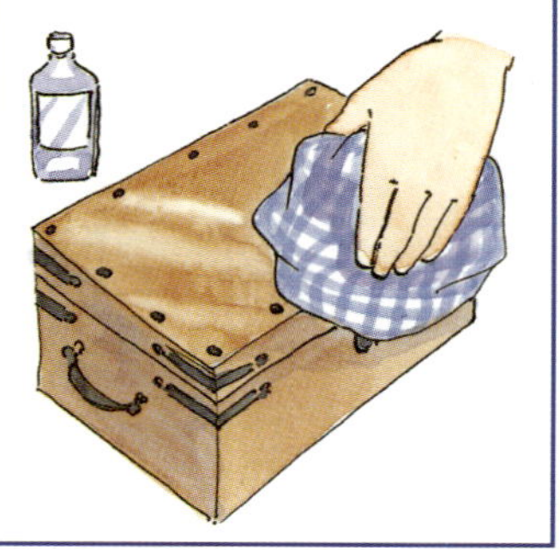

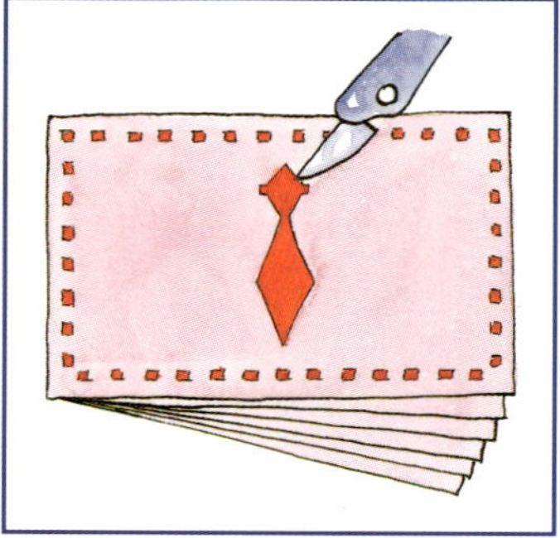

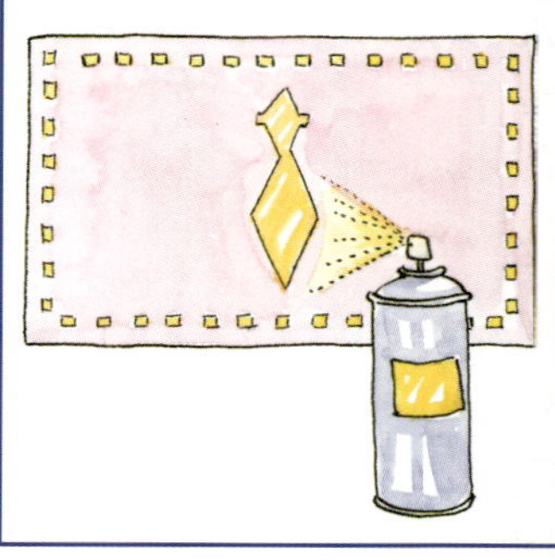

1 *Use turpentine on a cloth to remove any traces of grease and dirt from the wooden box, and allow to dry thoroughly.*

2 *Photocopy the template on page 52 six times and then, following the diagrams opposite, cut out each of the red sections to create six stencils that will layer up to complete the final design.*

3 *Take the first stencil and lightly spray the back with glue. Stick this to the top of your box. Use the gold spray paint to lightly spray over the stencil, concentrating on the cut-out sections. Allow to dry.*

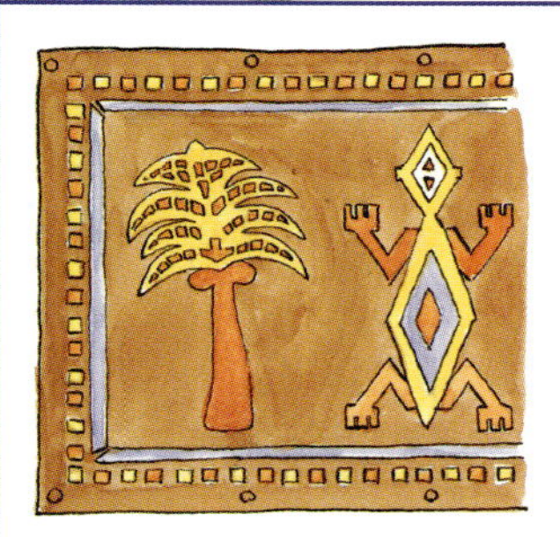

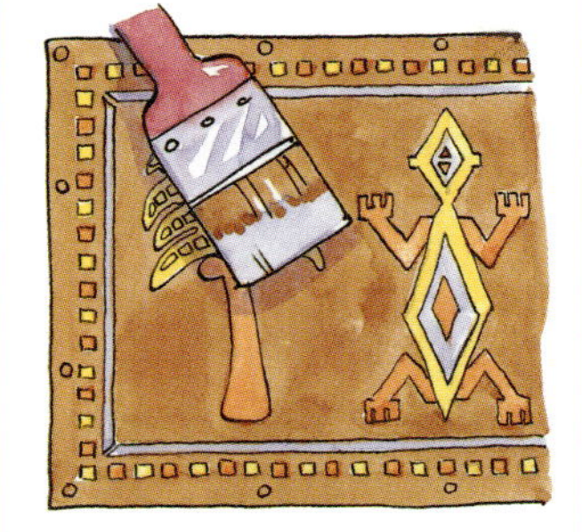

4 Take the remaining stencils and repeat the process again with the different colors, allowing time for the paint to dry in between each application.

5 When you have finished your design and it has completely dried, cover with a coat of acrylic varnish, as this will protect the design from scratches and scrapes.

Warning: Use spray paints in a well-ventilated area and mask the box and surrounding area.

Tip: When using spray paints, always spray at least 12 inches away from the stencil using an even pressure. Two thin coats are better than one thick coat, which could saturate the area, causing the paint to bleed under the stencil.

STENCIL CUTTING DIAGRAMS

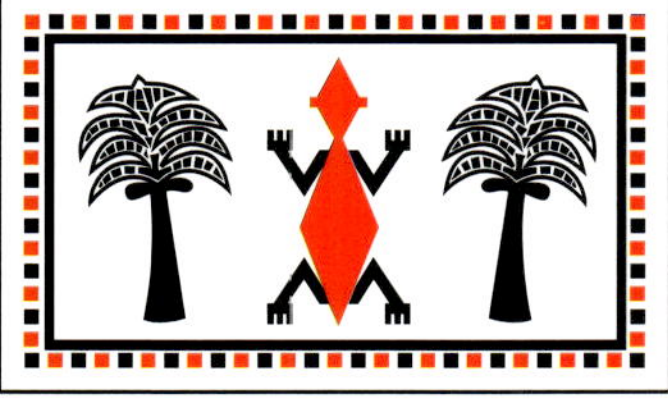

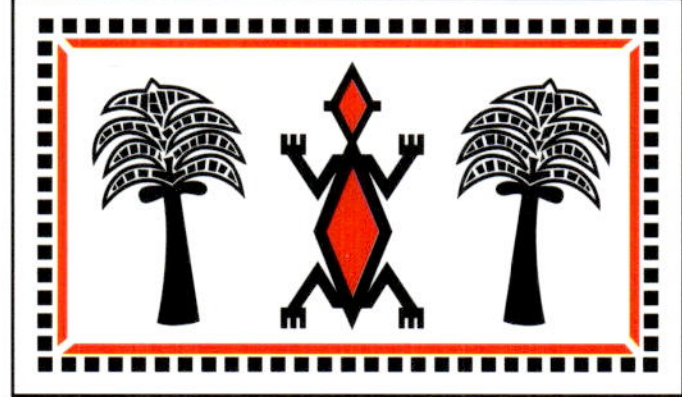

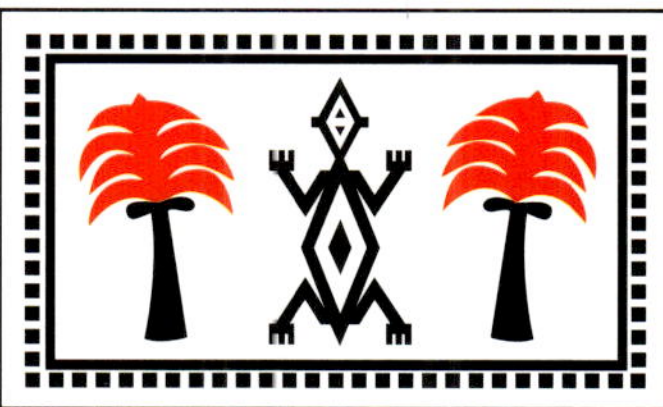

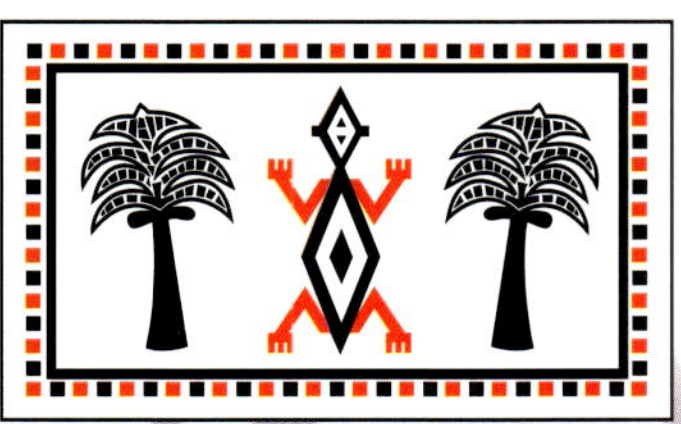

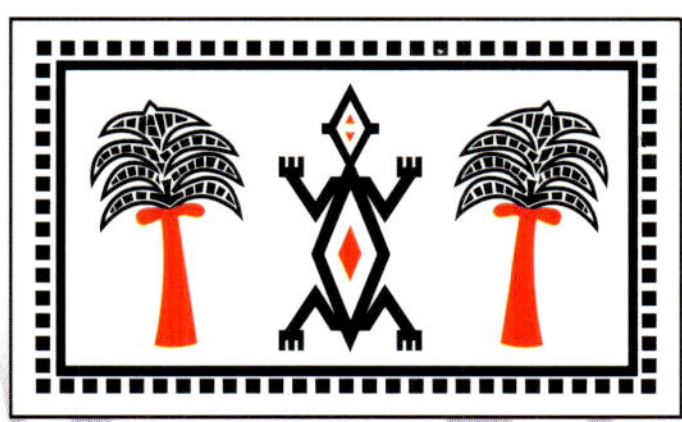

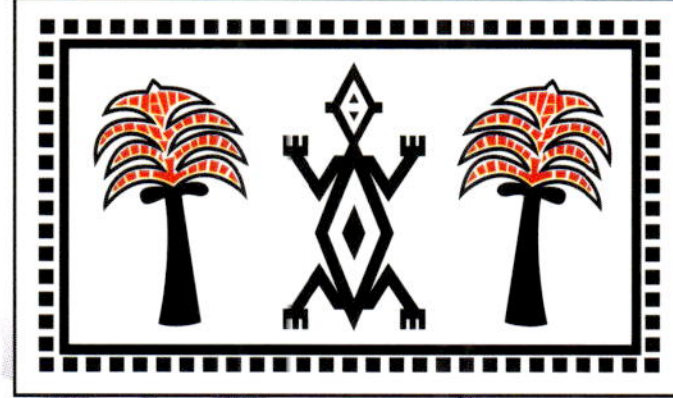

TEMPLATE AND COLOR GUIDE

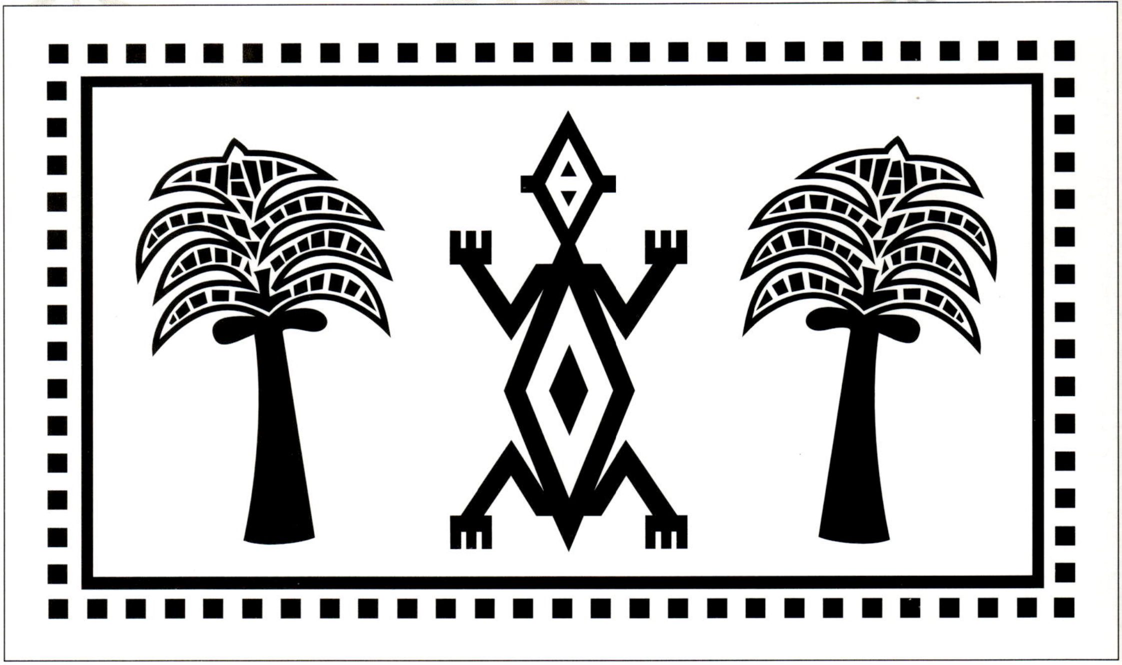

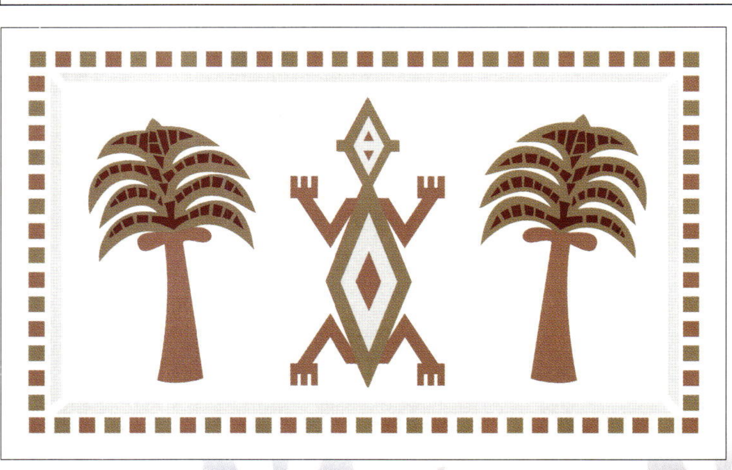

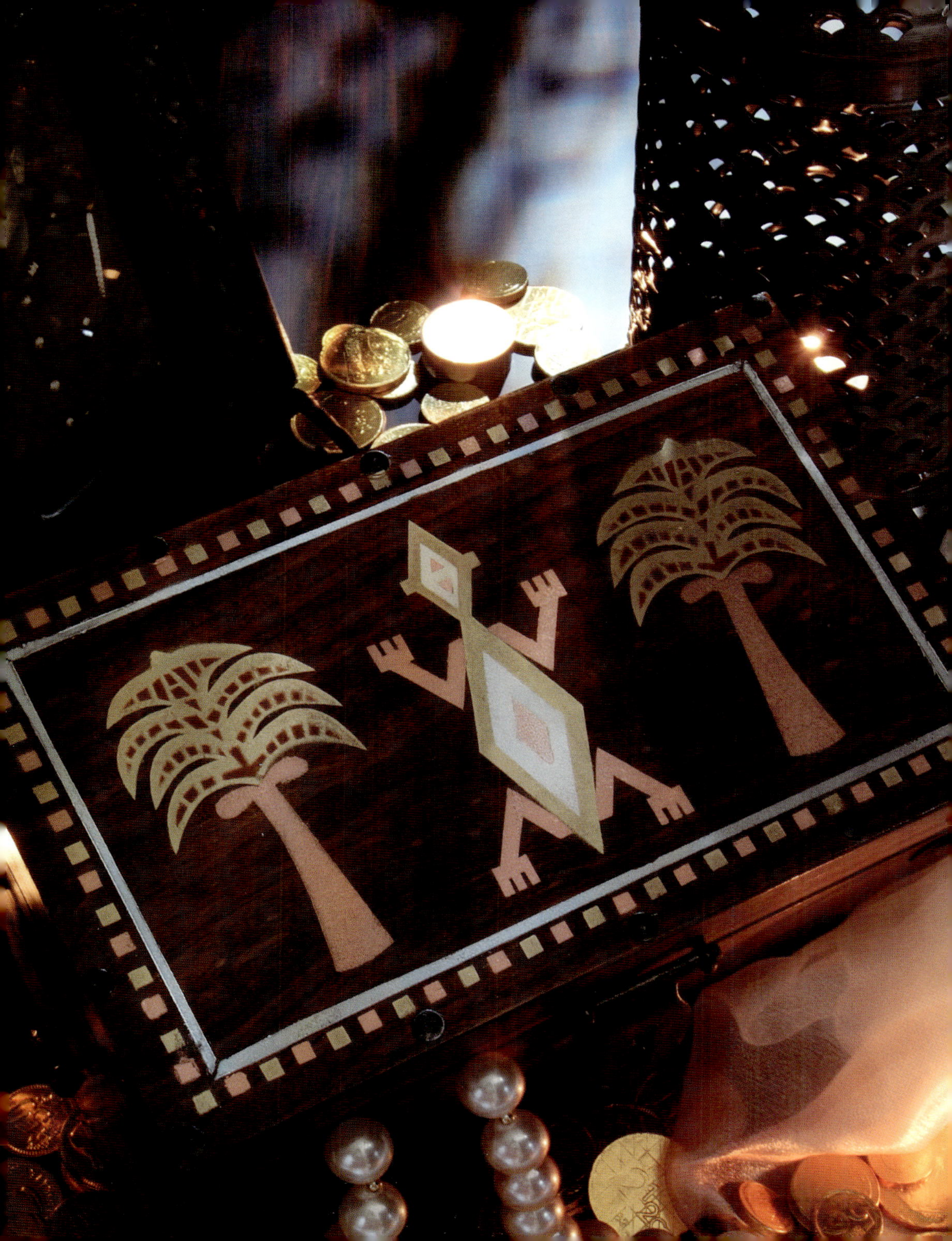

Ideas for the Future

Done well, stencil art can work wonders on a room. But you should proceed with caution as there are a number of things to think about before starting a project.

An easy mistake to make is to fall in love with a design and forget that it is not suited to the room you are about to design. Plant motifs may look good in the living room, but that does not mean they will look good in the dining room. Secondly, always consider those with whom you share your house and try to avoid making designs that are either too feminine or too masculine. Thirdly, be as confident as you can be that you will like the design when it's complete. Stenciling, though rewarding, is time-consuming, and so it is vital that you are pleased with the final design.

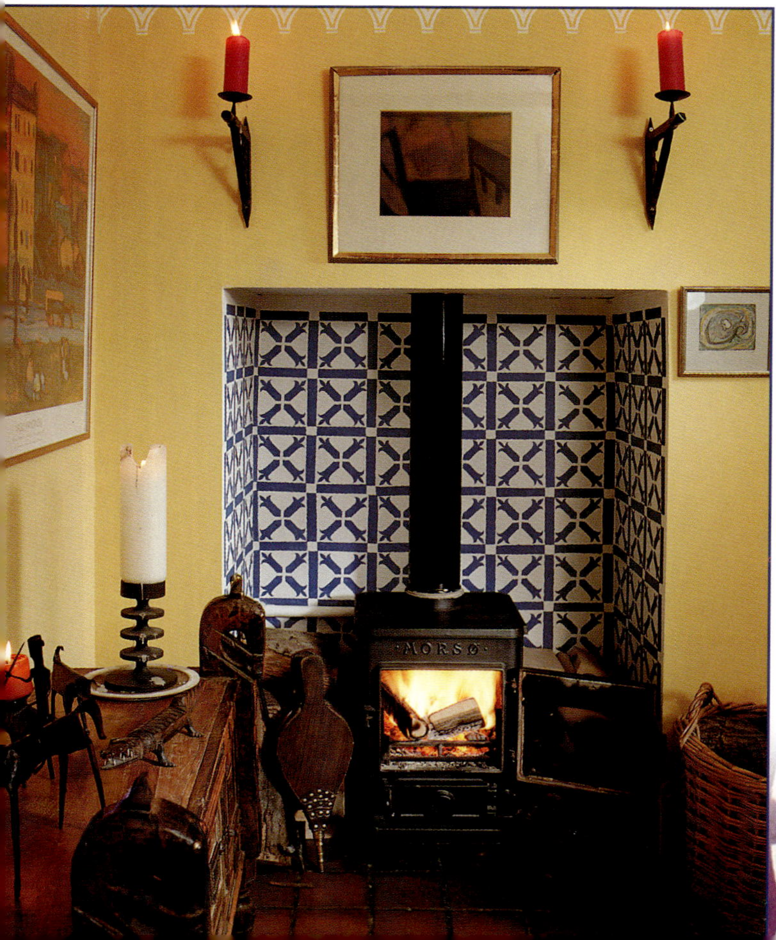

Kitchen

Old kitchen units can be revitalized with some stencil art. Designs incorporating brightly-colored fruit often work well here, as they create a sense that the room is abundantly full of health and life.

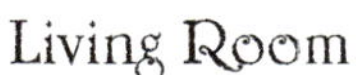

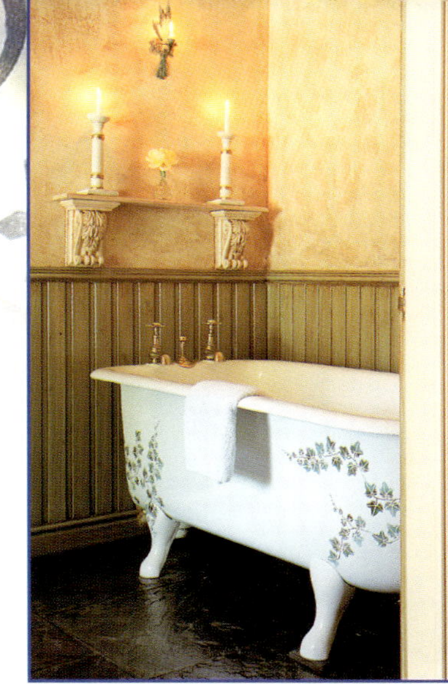

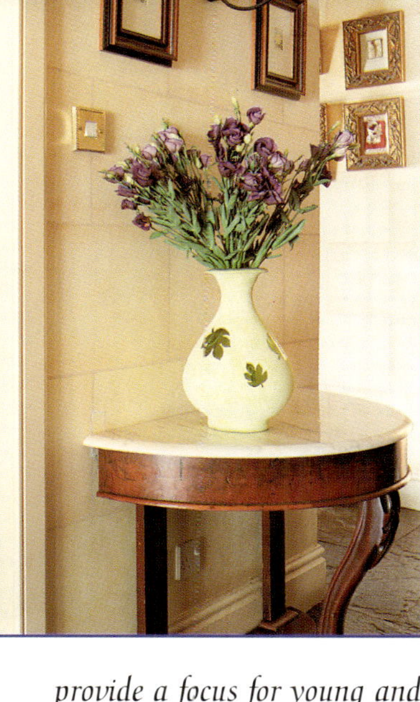

Living Room

As its name suggests, this is the room where you are likely to spend most of your time. As such, it is better to have a design that will help you relax. Use soothing colors such as light blues and greens. Neutral designs, such as fleurs-de-lys and crests at dado rail height can be appealing.

Dining Room

Although, like the kitchen, this room is associated with food, a more somber approach is appropriate. Simple abstract designs high up on the wall, sensitively executed with soft colors, can work as well as decorative work molded in stucco.

Bedroom

The bedroom is another room in which you need to be able to relax so, once again, designs using soft colors are appropriate. For a touch of subtlety, you may prefer to decorate the room's furniture only, and leave the walls alone. Unfussy floral designs and simple motifs are sure to cheer up chests of drawers, wardrobes, and the like. Alternatively, why not try a fresher approach and experiment with geometric shapes and blocks of color?

Nursery

Stencil art is great for the nursery. Repeated designs using your children's favorite characters will not only help them to feel safe but also provide a focus for young and inquiring minds.

Bathroom

Bathrooms, are, of course, associated with water. Common designs incorporate dolphins and turtles, but you could try shells or seahorses. You should also look around for inspiration—Japanese prints could easily be adapted to form the basis of a stencil. Don't restrict your designs to the wall in this room either; a reclaimed, free-standing bathtub could be transformed with an inspired design. Colors should be kept low-key and relaxing.

Floral Templates

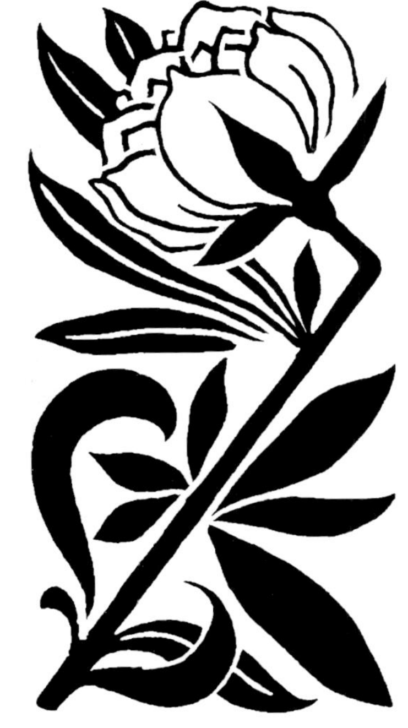

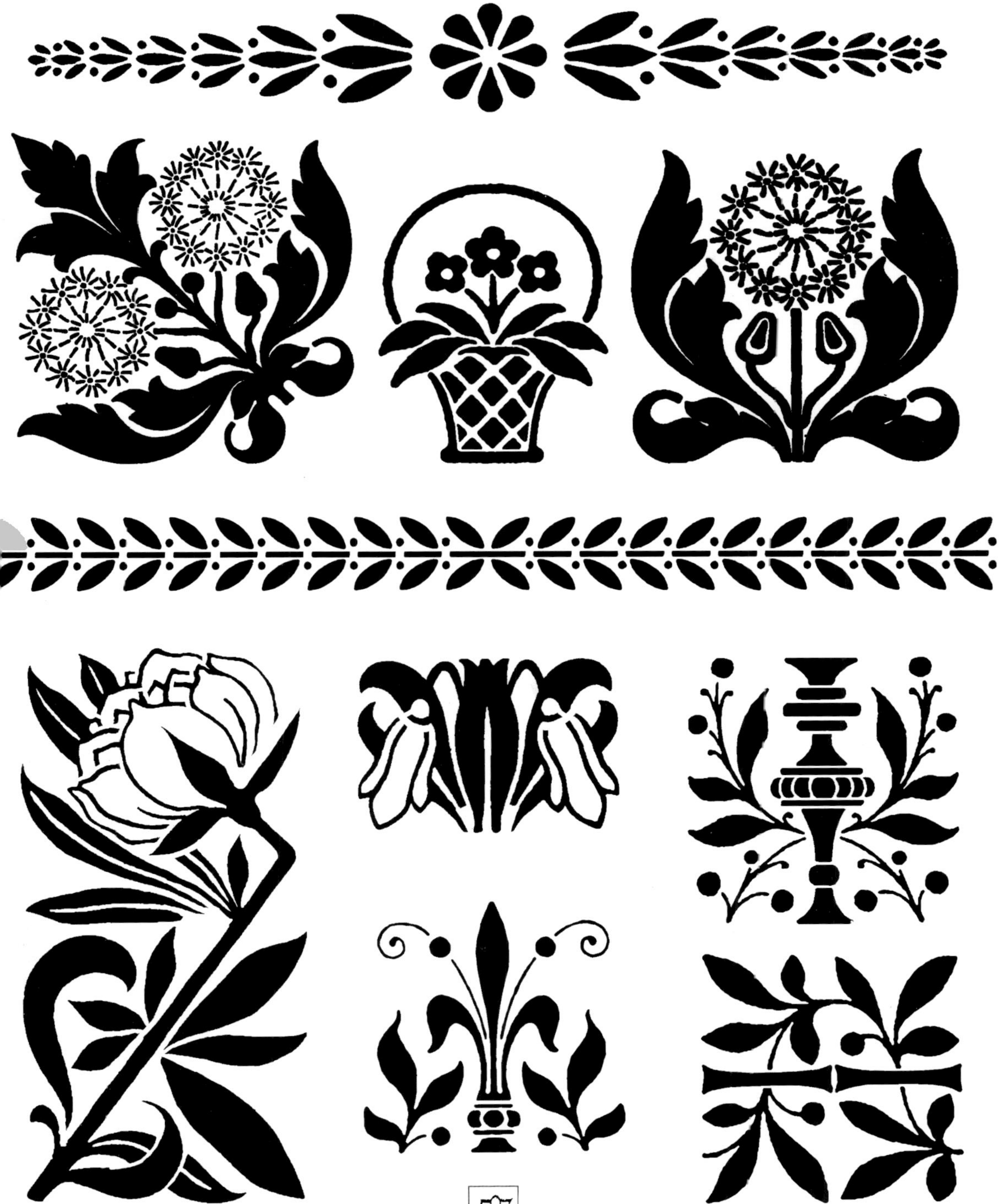

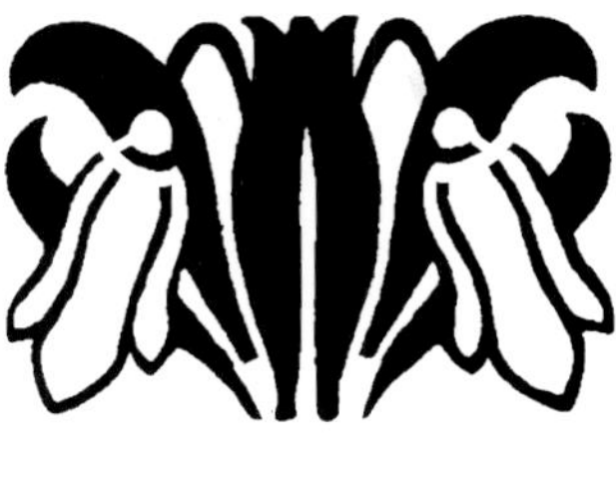

Vine Templates

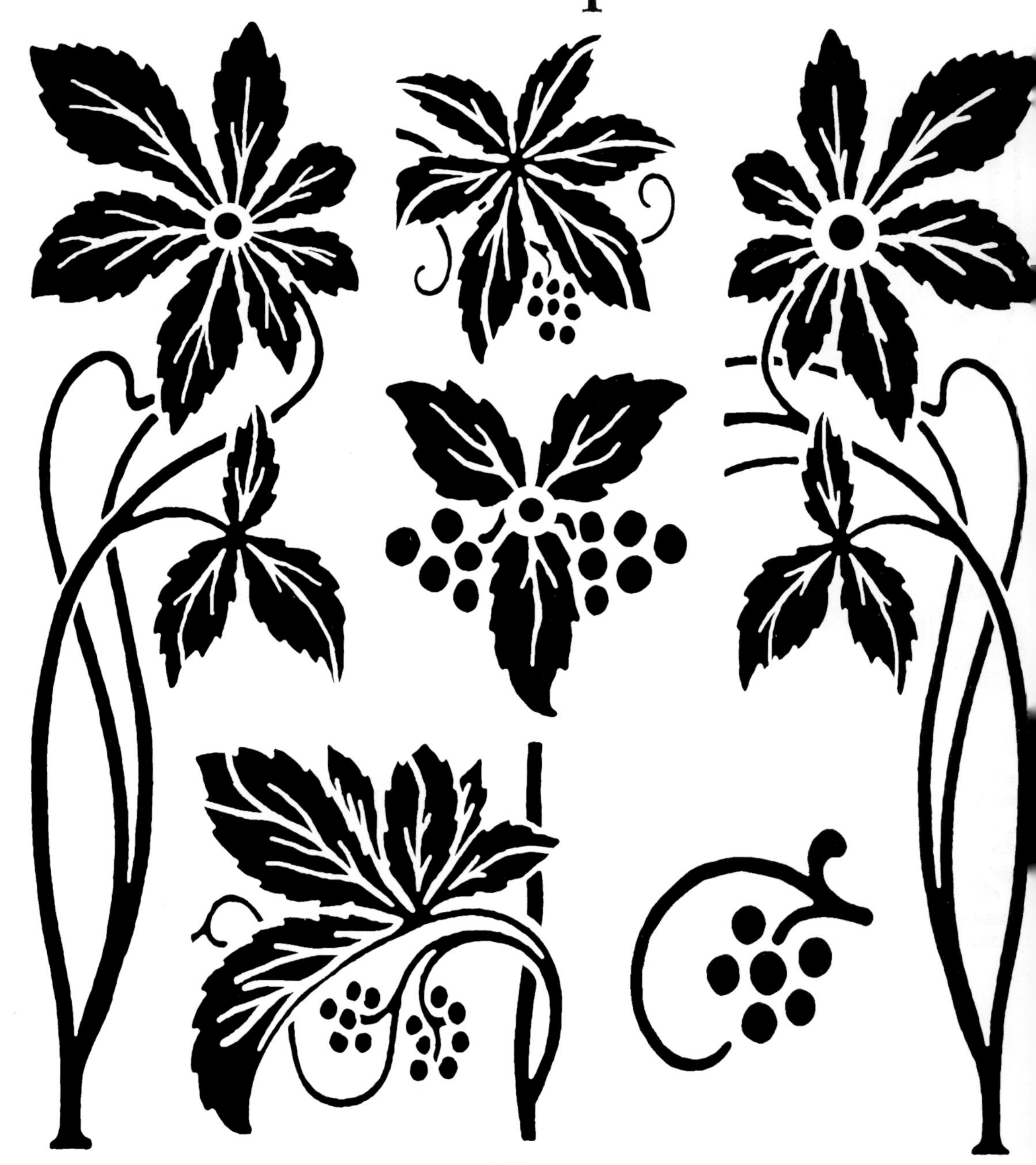

Grecian Templates

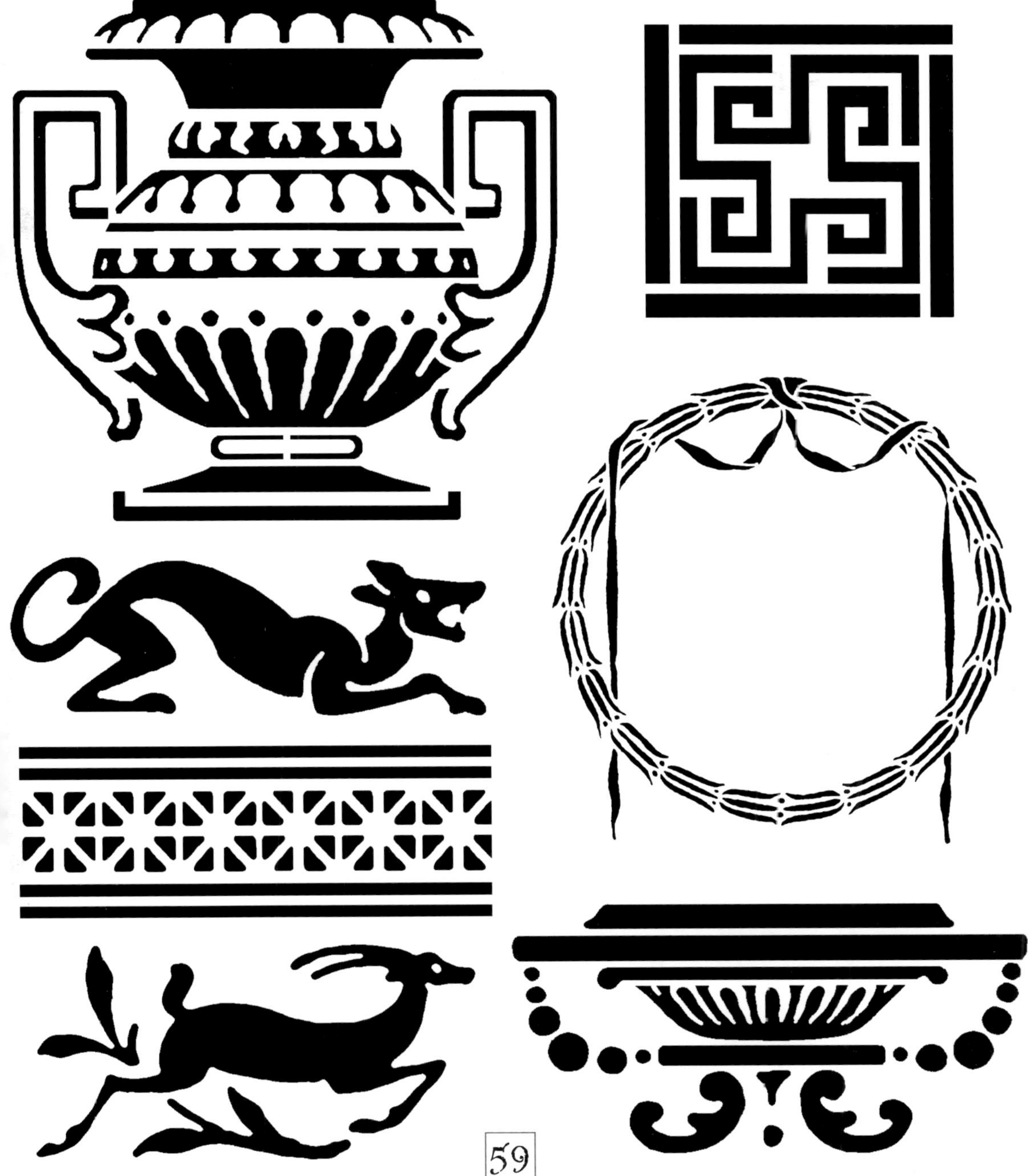

Icons and Symbols

Border Templates

Nouveau Templates

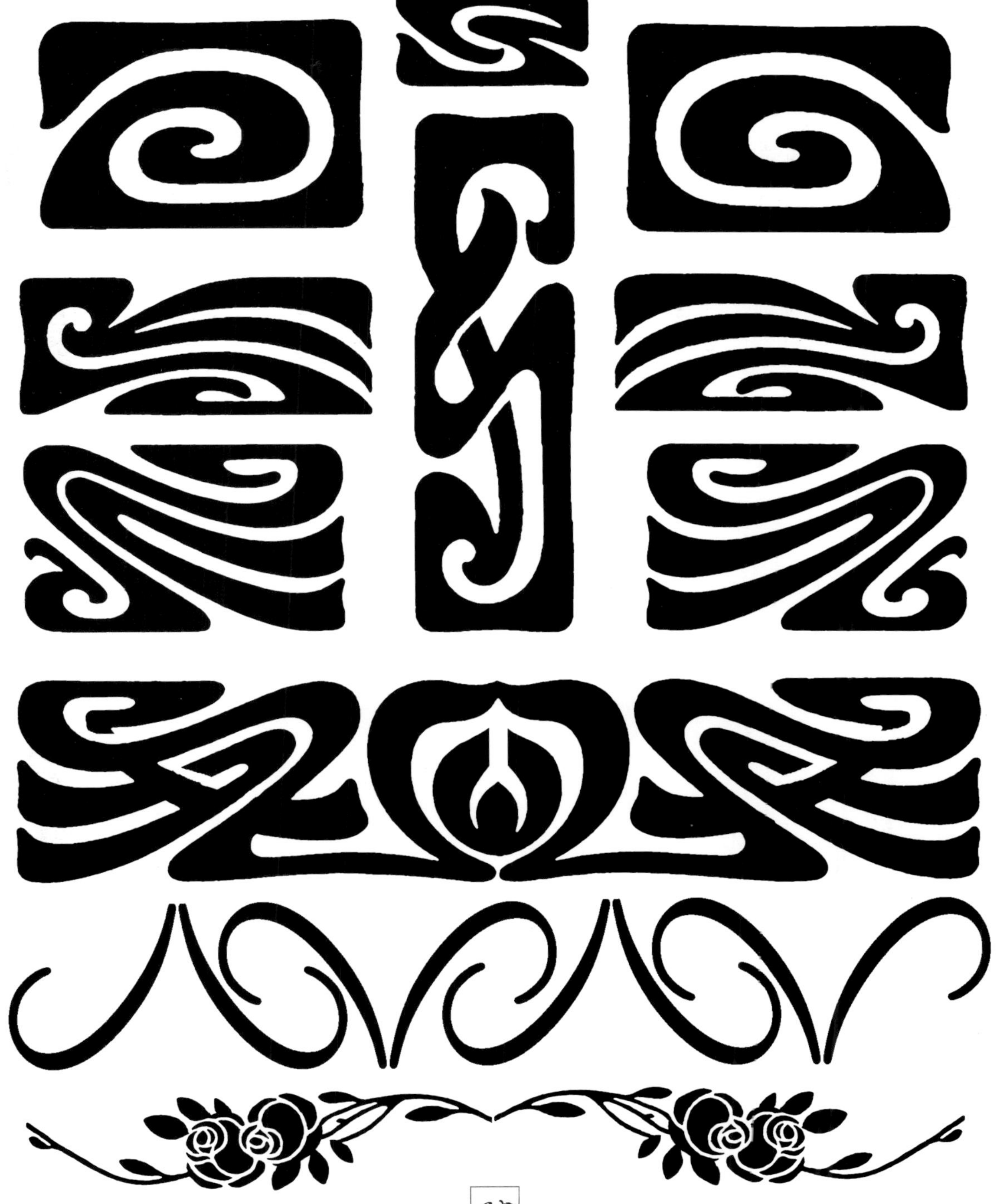

Conclusion

Completing the array of projects in this book should have shown you the versatility of stenciling. Using just acrylic paint, you can create imaginative and memorable designs.

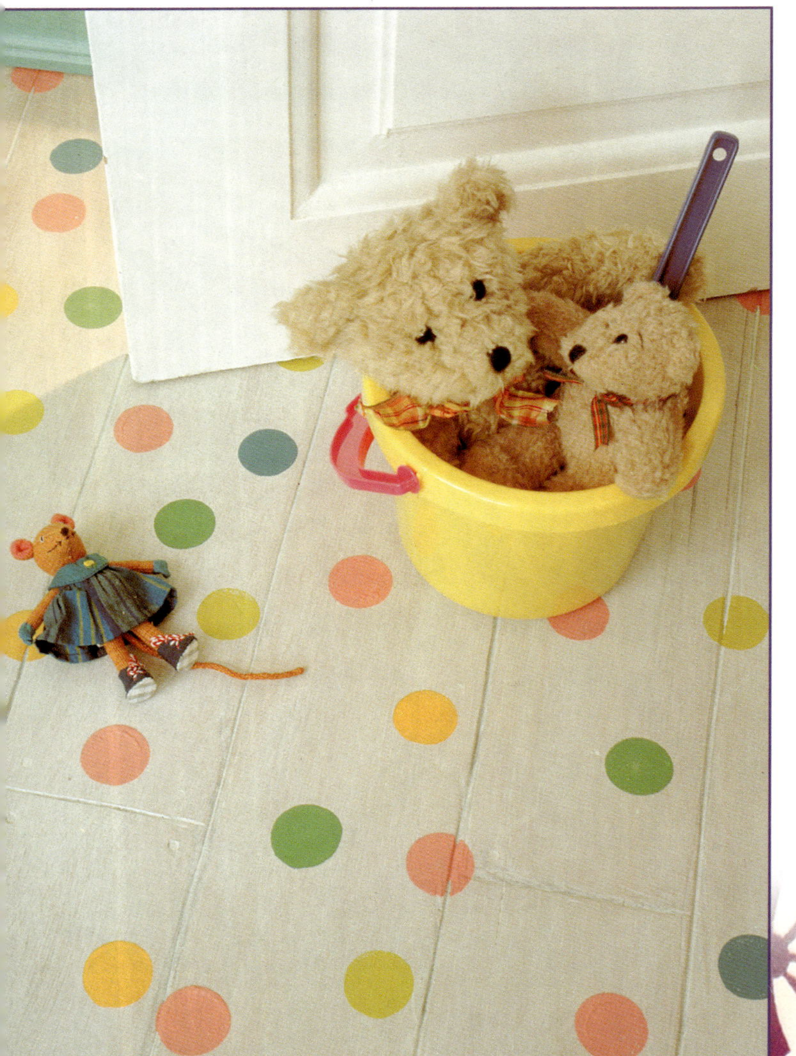

As your skills improve, you should try to broaden your supply of materials, and try out more specialist paints to get even better results.

Take note of your surroundings, look for inspiration from nature, magazines, or television, or try following some of our future project ideas.

Whatever task you take on next, it's sure to be just the beginning of a creative interest that will keep you occupied for years to come.

Picture Credits

Key: top - t; middle - m; bottom - b; left - l; right - r.

Abode Interiors Picture Library: 9(t); 10(m); 17; 54(bl); 55(tr); 64(bl).